PLEBES

PLEBES

THE CARTOON GUIDE FOR COLLEGE GUYS

by L.T. Horton
of The Onion®

**Andrews McMeel
Publishing**

Kansas City

01 02 03 04 05 BAH 10 9 8 7 6 5 4 3 2 1

ISBN: 0-7407-1851-7

Library of Congress Catalog Card Number: 2001087673

──── ATTENTION: SCHOOLS AND BUSINESSES ────

Andrews McMeel books are available at quantity discounts with bulk purchase for educational, business, or sales promotional use. For information, please write to: Special Sales Department, Andrews McMeel Publishing, 4520 Main Street, Kansas City, Missouri 64111.

WHAT IS A PLEBE?
A SCIENTIFIC INQUIRY

IN EXPERIMENTAL STUDIES, ISOLATED CONTROL GROUPS EXPOSED TO KEGS OF BEER DISPLAY NO SIGNIFICANT BEHAVIORAL CHANGE.

A PLEBE CAN EASILY BE IDENTIFIED BY THE BASEBALL CAP, WORN BACKWARDS AT A 135° ANGLE FROM THE CURVATURE OF THE HEAD.

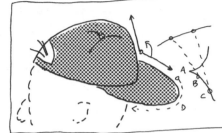

A PACK OF PLEBES, ON THE OTHER HAND, EXHIBITS A MARKEDLY DIFFERENT RESPONSE.

OOOW!
BEER!!
WOO!
WOOF! WOOF! WOOF!

THE SIMIAN GAIT OF THE COMMON NORTH AMERICAN PLEBE IS EVIDENCED WHEN JUXTAPOSED WITH MODELS OF BOTH HUMAN AND CHIMP.

HUMAN   PLEBE   CHIMP

ALSO LIKE THE CHIMP AND OTHER BRUTES, THE PLEBE IS PRIMALLY DRIVEN TO THOUGHTS OF REPRODUCTION.

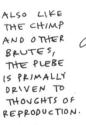

THESE CHICKS THEY GOT FOR FEBRUARY ARE ALMOST AS AWESOME AS MY BUD GIRLS!

NOW THAT YOU BETTER UNDERSTAND THEM, SEE IF YOU CAN SPOT THE PLEBE.

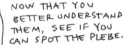

MALE BONDING
THE PLEBES WAY

BONDING FOR A FEW MINUTES

"HEY, DUDE— YER WALLET'S FALLIN' OUTTA YER PANTS"

"WHOA— THANKS, DUDE"

BONDING FOR A DAY

"HEY— I'M OUTTA SHAVING CREAM— ANYBODY GOT SOME?"

"SURE... HERE YA GO, DUDE— USE MINE."

BONDING FOR THE WEEKEND

"WAIT— IS THAT MY BEER? OR IS THAT ONE MINE?"

"I DUNNO, DUDE. WHICHEVER. YOU DON'T HAVE ANY INCUR'BLE DISEASES DO YA?"

BONDING FOR THE SEMESTER

"HEY— AIN'T YOU IN MY PSYCH 103 CLASS?"

"YEAH— THAT CLASS BITES, HUH?"

BONDING FOR 4 YEARS OF COLLEGE

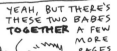

"OH— AWESOME CENTERFOLD, DUDE!"

"YEAH, BUT THERE'S THESE TWO BABES **TOGETHER** A FEW MORE PAGES IN..."

BONDING FOR LIFE

"HEY, DUDE, SOMEBODY PUKED ON MY BUNK— CAN I SLEEP IN YOURS?"

"**NO WAY!!** WELL, I S'PPOSE, LONG AS YOU DON'T TRY NOTHIN' FUNNY"

6

GET A MINIMUM-WAGE JOB
AND SEE HOW FAST YOU CAN LOSE IT!

YOU'RE OUTTA HERE, BUSTER!

YOU'RE HISTORY, PAL!

YOU'RE FIRED! I MEAN IT!

YOU'VE DISGRACED THE BURGER BUCKET NAME. TAKE A HIKE, BUDDY!

FRY COOK

WHENEVER YOUR BOSS SAYS, "WOULD YOU LIKE ANYTHING ELSE WITH THAT TODAY?" TO A CUSTOMER, LOB A BACON-DOUBLE CHEESE-BURGER AND KNOCK OFF HIS PAPER HAT.

JANITOR

SWEEP AND MOP ALL THE DIRT & DEBRIS INTO YOUR BOSS'S OFFICE, FILL HIS WATER COOLER WITH AMMONIA, AND SMUDGE THE FAMILY PORTRAITS ON HIS DESK WITH CRUSTED EXCREMENT FROM THE BATHROOM.

WAITER

ARRIVE AT A TABLE OF HUNGRY, EAGER PATRONS WITH A BIG PLATTER OF FOOD, SET IT DOWN NEARBY, THEN PLACE A HANDFUL OF DEAD COCKROACHES IN FRONT OF EACH PERSON, PICK UP THE TRAY AND WALK TO A DIFFERENT TABLE.

OFFICE GO-FER

EVERY TIME YOU MAKE A RUN TO THE XEROX ROOM, RETURN ONLY WITH COPIES OF YOUR BUTT CHEEKS.

HOW TO LOOK COOL

PLEBES' GUIDE TO SPRING FASHION FOR 19-YEAR-OLD BUCKS

CAP
WHITE, WITH A CLASSY, CONVERSATION-STARTING EMBLEM ON THE FRONT AND A SIZE-ADJUSTMENT STRAP IN BACK. WHEN WORN BACKWARDS, THIS CAUSES YOUR HAIR TO PROTRUDE PROMINENTLY THROUGH THE HOLE, GIVING YOU AN APPEALING, I-DON'T-NEED-TO-CARE-IF-MY-HAIR-GETS-MUSSED LOOK.

SMILE LIKE MR. ED WHENEVER ONE OF YOUR FRIENDS MAKES A LEWD COMMENT ABOUT SEXUAL INTERCOURSE, DRINKING, HOMOSEXUALS, OR WOMEN.

T-SHIRT
WITH A HIP, STYLISH DESIGN ON IT. GIRLS' EYES WILL LIGHT UP IF YOU SAY YOU GOT IT SOME-WHERE EXOTIC, LIKE THE L.A. OUTLET.

SHADES
SUGGEST FOREBODING, REBELLIOUS, CAPTIVATING EYES THAT MUST BE CONCEALED, LEST THEY HYPNOTIZE EVERY WOMAN WHO CATCHES A GLIMPSE OF THEM. ($5 AT WALGREEN'S.)

FLIGHT JACKET
BROWN, WITH SIMULATED "WORN" LOOK. YOUR FRIENDS WILL THINK YOU DOGFIGHT COMMIES WHEN YOU'RE NOT HANGING OUT WITH THE GANG IN THE DORM LOUNGE.

JEANS
FAKE-BLEACHED, THAT BUNDLE UP DOWN AT THE FEET. THEY GIVE YOU THAT RUGGED, OUTDOORSY, I-BUY-THE-SAME-PANTS-EVERYBODY-ELSE-DOES LOOK.

BASKETBALL SHOES
WHITE, WITH TONGUE AND SIDES STICKING OUT LIKE FLAPS. COUPLED WITH YOUR RUMPLED PANT LEGS, THEY GIVE YOU A BIG-FOOTED "ALLEY OOP" LOOK GIRLS CAN'T RESIST.

LH

HOW TO GET A REAL-WORLD JOB AFTER COLLEGE

PRINT UP A RESUMÉ AT KINKO'S. PUT A FANCY BORDER AROUND IT, AND WRITE YOUR NAME IN BIG GOTHIC LETTERS

Gus Bozwel

AND REMEMBER: USE ACTION VERBS!

EXPERIENCE
HEAVED SNOW FROM NEIGHBOR'S WALK
HURLED HAMBURGER PATTIES WITH SPATULA AT WENDY'S

EDUCATION
WHISKED THROUGH COLLEGE ON PARENTS' MONEY AND DIDN'T LEARN DIDDLY POOP.

GOALS
TO INVIGORATE THE SOCK-MARKETING INDUSTRY.

ALONG WITH YOUR RESUMÉ, SEND A COVER LETTER PRINTED ON FINE COTTON-BOND PAPER WITH A MACINTOSH LASER PRINTER— YOUR PROSPECTIVE EMPLOYERS WILL BE TOUCHED TO KNOW YOU SENT THEM THE SAME MASS-PRODUCED LETTER YOU SENT TO 300 OTHER COMPANIES.

AT YOUR INTERVIEW:

WEAR HARD SHOES. DON'T CHEW GUM.

WHAT CAN YOU OFFER SHIFTMAN & LEAMAN ADVERTISING?

I WAS ON MY HIGH-SCHOOL DEBATE SQUAD.

I LEARNED ORGANIZATIONAL, LEADERSHIP, AND RESPONSIBILITY SKILLS WORKING AT DAIRY QUEEN.

MY MOM SPENT $400 ON THIS SUIT.

BEFORE YOU KNOW IT, YOU'LL BE LEADING THE EXCITING 9-TO-5 WORKER-BEE LIFE DEPICTED BY YOUR FAVORITE STARS ON TV SHOWS LIKE "THIRTY-SOMETHING," AND HIT MOVIES LIKE "WORKING GIRL."

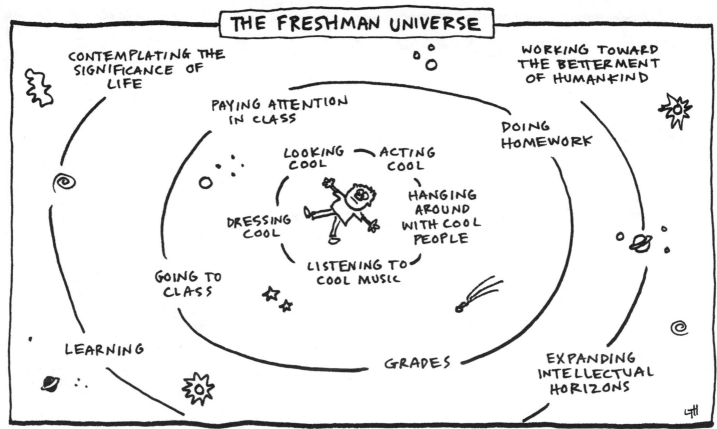

THE FRESHMAN UNIVERSE

CONTEMPLATING THE SIGNIFICANCE OF LIFE

WORKING TOWARD THE BETTERMENT OF HUMANKIND

PAYING ATTENTION IN CLASS

DOING HOMEWORK

LOOKING COOL — ACTING COOL

HANGING AROUND WITH COOL PEOPLE

DRESSING COOL

GOING TO CLASS

LISTENING TO COOL MUSIC

LEARNING

GRADES

EXPANDING INTELLECTUAL HORIZONS

OUT OF THE PICTURE: STAYING ABREAST OF CURRENT EVENTS, KEEPING UP CORRESPONDENCE WITH GRANDPARENTS.

BECOME A GREAT PHILOSOPHER!

YOU'VE STUDIED ALL THE FAMOUS PHILOSOPHERS IN COLLEGE. THE NEXT STEP IS TO ADD **YOURSELF** TO THEIR RANKS. *YOUR NAME WILL LIVE IN HISTORY!*

PLATO BELIEVED THE ABSTRACT IDEAL IS THE TRUEST REALITY.

DESCARTES SAID, "I THINK, THEREFORE I AM."

MARXISM POSITED THAT HUMAN ACTION IS MOTIVATED BY SOCIOECONOMICS.

HOW HARD CAN IT BE?

JUST WRITE DOWN WHAT YOU THINK ABOUT LIFE, THE WORLD, HUMAN BEHAVIOR, ETC., IN A THICK BORING BOOK AND GIVE IT A REALLY HIGH FALUTIN TITLE, LIKE "THE STRUCTURE OF REASON," "SOCIALIZATION AND THOUGHT," OR "A TREATISE ON THE RELEVANCE OF LOGIC."

DEAN TETFORDISM

"IF YOU REALLY WANT SOMETHING IN LIFE, I THINK YOU'LL GET IT— IF YOU WORK REALLY HARD AT IT."

SUSY FREEDMANISM

"I THINK PEOPLE ARE GENERALLY PRETTY NICE INSIDE, IF YOU GIVE 'EM HALF A CHANCE."

NICK WALSHISM

"I GUESS I BELIEVE IN GOD. I DON'T KNOW. I GUESS WE'LL FIND OUT WHEN WE DIE."

TERRY DUNBYISM

"I LOVE HORSES!"

LtH

AND SOMEDAY YOUR PHILOSOPHY WILL BE TAUGHT IN COLLEGE CLASSES ALONGSIDE THE GREAT THINKERS OF HISTORY...

...SO, AS OPPOSED TO KIERKEGAARD, PUTZFIELD BELIEVES **BEER** IS AN IMPORTANT FACTOR IN THE HUMAN CONDITION....

ADVENTURES IN PARTY-TIME URINATION

ELEMENTARY SKILL-LEVEL

WAIT IN LINE FOR SEVERAL MINUTES TO USE THE BATHROOM.

INTERMEDIATE SKILL-LEVEL

YOU'RE STUCK WITH A DOOR THAT DOESN'T SHUT OR LOCK. TRY TO HOLD IT SHUT AND STILL GET CLOSE ENOUGH TO THE TOILET.

JUST FOR FUN...

"CROSS STREAMS." (EXCELLENT FOR MALE BONDING.)

ADVANCED SKILL-LEVEL

THE BATHROOM LINE IS TOO LONG AND YOU CAN'T WAIT. THE BUSHES OUTSIDE SHOULD PROVIDE ADEQUATE COVER. KEEP OUT OF SIGHT OF CARS AND PASSERS-BY.

MASTER SKILL-LEVEL

YOU JUST CAN'T HOLD IT IN. WITH SUFFICIENT DIVERSION, RELIEVE YOURSELF IN A BEER CUP, AND PLACE IT SLYLY ON AN OUT-OF-THE-WAY SHELF.

LIVE THE ROMANTIC LIFE OF
THE DORM LOUNGE POOL PLAYER

IMAGINE YOU'RE THE JAMES BOND OF THE WORLD OF POOL!

SHOOT POOL IN A SMOKE-FILLED HOLLOW WHERE SOMEBODY ELSE ALWAYS KNOWS MORE ABOUT OFFICIAL POOL RULES THAN YOU

MAKE LIFE-LONG FRIENDS WITH OTHER MEDIOCRE POOL PLAYERS WHOSE NAMES YOU'LL NEVER KNOW.

PLAY FOR MONEY AND RISK RUNNING OUT OF QUARTERS YOU'D SAVED FOR THE LAUNDRY

TRY YOUR DARNEDEST TO PUT THE BALLS IN THEIR HOLES, BUT WHEN YOU MISS BY SEVERAL INCHES, CURSE DISBELIEVINGLY

SIZING UP YOUR OPPONENT

SIGN	MESSAGE
HE RUBS CHALK ON HIS CUE	HE'S PROBABLY PLAYED BEFORE AND WILL WIN. DON'T PLAY FOR MONEY
HE ASKS HOW THE BALLS SHOULD BE ORGANIZED IN THE TRIANGLE RACK	PRETEND YOU KNOW, AND PLAY FOR MONEY
HE BRINGS HIS OWN CUE	GO HOME

INTIMIDATE AND WEAKEN YOUR OPPONENT WHILE HE SHOOTS BY STRIKING ONE OF THESE POOL-PLAYER STANCES THAT WILL MAKE YOU LOOK COOL.

—YOU CAN BE A CAMPUS CHRISTIAN—

LEARN HOW TO:

- SMILE VACANTLY WHEN PASSING OUT PAMPHLETS

- SMILE VACANTLY WHEN RECITING INSPIRATIONAL VERSE

- SMILE VACANTLY WHEN CONFRONTED BY FOUL-MOUTHED HECKLERS

- SMILE VACANTLY WHEN RELIEVING YOUR BOWELS

JUST MEMORIZE THESE KEY PHRASES:

"DO YOU KNOW THE LORD?"

"JESUS LOVES YOU"

"HAVE A NICE DAY"

"YOU'RE GOING TO HELL"

TRAPPED IN A DISCUSSION WITH A LEFT-WING AGNOSTIC? EASY! JUST REPEAT THIS SENTENCE ENDLESSLY WITHOUT PAUSING:

"CHRIST DIED ON THE CROSS TO SAVE YOU FROM SIN"

HINT: LOCK YOURSELF IN YOUR ROOM AND MASTURBATE FURIOUSLY... GOD WILL FORGIVE YOU EVERY TIME!

LTH

GOT A GRIPE?
WRITE YOUR STATE REPRESENTATIVE
PLEBES' GUIDE TO RESPONSIBLE CITIZENSHIP

LIKE EVERY RESPONSIBLE CITIZEN, YOU HAVE GRIPES, CONCERNS AND NEEDS. JUST JOT THEM DOWN...

BEER SHOULD BE GIVEN OUT FREE BY THE GOVERNMENT!

PANHANDLERS SHOULD BE ROUNDED UP AND GASSED!

I WANT WORLD PEACE NOW!

I'M SICK OF THESE DAMN ZITS!

GET YOUR REPRESENTATIVE'S ADDRESS FROM THE PHONE BOOK AND MAIL THE LETTER PROMPTLY.

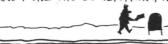

YOU'LL FEEL WARM WITH PATRIOTISM.

IN A FEW WEEKS YOU'LL GET A FORM LETTER THAT THANKS YOU FOR SHARING YOUR THOUGHTS

A FORM LETTER — THAT MEANS THE BUM DIDN'T EVEN READ YOUR LETTER!

BE PERSISTENT. FIND OUT WHERE HE LIVES, THEN GET SHIT-FACED DRUNK AND HOLLER YOUR THOUGHTS OUTSIDE HIS WINDOW AT 3 a.m.

OR WRITE ANOTHER LETTER. ONLY THIS TIME, TELL HIM YOU KNOW WHERE HIS CHILDREN GO TO SCHOOL.

DeaR RePR

OR SNEAK INTO HIS OFFICE AT NIGHT AND PAINT YOUR REQUESTS ON HIS WALLS WITH SHEEPS' BLOOD.

I WAN

IN NO TIME, YOUR REPRESENTATIVE WILL GIVE YOU A PERSONAL REPLY, RECOGNIZING YOU AS A VALUED CONSTITUENT.

YOU MAY EVEN GET YOUR PICTURE ON THE FRONT PAGE OF YOUR DORM NEWSLETTER

WITTE WORLD

AND ALL FOR JUST DOING YOUR CIVIC DUTY!

WHAT'S YOUR MAJOR?

A LOOK AT HOW YOUR UNDERGRADUATE DEGREE CAN FORETELL WHERE YOU MIGHT END UP IN LIFE...

MAJOR	1 YEAR AFTER COLLEGE	5 YEARS AFTER COLLEGE	15 YEARS AFTER COLLEGE	30 YEARS AFTER COLLEGE	40 YEARS AFTER COLLEGE	EVENTUAL PERSONALITY
COMPUTER ENGINEERING	FRY COOK AT A&W	DATA-ENTRY TECHNICIAN	ASSISTANT PROGRAMMER	FLOW-CHART TEAM COORDINATOR	ASSISTANT SUPERVISOR OF HARDWARE DIVISION	BAD BREATH, NO SENSE OF HUMOR
JOURNALISM	FRY COOK AT A&W	REPORTER FOR THE BEAVER COUNTY TIDBIT	MANAGING EDITOR OF THE BEAVER COUNTY TIDBIT	EDITOR OF THE BEAVER COUNTY TIDBIT	PUBLISHER OF THE BEAVER COUNTY TIDBIT	SAD AND HATEFUL. ONLY JOY COMES FROM FINDING TYPOS IN THE NEW YORK TIMES
PHILOSOPHY	FRY COOK AT A&W	BACK FOR A MASTERS DEGREE IN PHILOSOPHY.	FRY COOK AT A&W	 BACK FOR A Ph.D. in PHILOSOPHY	FRY COOK AT A&W	BITTER, UNFULFILLED INTELLECTUAL, AND A DAMN GOOD FRY COOK

TURN YOUR DORMITORY INTO A LUCRATIVE REAL-ESTATE INVESTMENT

ACT AS AN UNLICENSED REAL-ESTATE BROKER, RENTING OUT ROOMS IN YOUR RESIDENCE HALL

PRINT UP NOTICES ON WHAT LOOKS LIKE OFFICIAL UNIVERSITY STATIONERY INFORMING TENANTS THAT YOU'RE THE NEW LANDLORD — MAKE IT SOUND LEGAL!

OFFICIAL UNIVERSITY HOUSING OFFICE NOTICE

Hey Tenants... Hereby send all your rent money from now on to Skip Grissome, room 310. We're completely serious! Be sure — make checks out to: S-K-I-P G-R-I-S-S-O-M-E

LOOK OUT DONALD TRUMP!

...TEN THOUSAND 20, TEN THOUSAND 30, TEN THOUSAND 40...WAIT... 50? AW, SHIT! ONE, TWO, THREE...

INSTITUTE FREQUENT RENT HIKES OF UP TO 200% — YOUR TENANTS' WELL-TO-DO PARENTS PAY ALL THE BILLS. THEY WON'T EVEN NOTICE THE INCREASES!

NEW FIDS

YOU NEED RENT MONEY, EH? 5000? 10,000? ALRIGHT, WHATEVER

WITH THE RENT MONEY YOU MAKE, FINANCE RENOVATIONS TO THE PROPERTY TO INCREASE ITS RESALE VALUE

SKIP'S LUXURY CONDOS

WE OFFER POOL LOUNGE LAUNDRY FACILITIES RESIDENT ADVISORS

SKIPS

THEN SELL IT TO A LARGE DEVELOPMENT COMPANY FOR AN OUTLANDISH PROFIT

BY THE TIME THEY FIND OUT YOU WEREN'T THE REAL OWNER, YOU'LL HAVE ALREADY CASHED THE CHECK!

I'M GONNA BUY A TRUCK FULL OF BEER!

LH

HOW TO SURVIVE YOUR FIRST YEAR OF COLLEGE

PLEBES OFFERS THIS HANDY LIVING-STYLE GUIDE TO NEW STUDENTS

WEAR YOUR SIMPSONS T-SHIRT WHEREVER YOU GO SO PEOPLE WILL KNOW YOU'RE IN THE VANGUARD OF POP-CULTURE HIPNESS

EAT 3 HEARTY MEALS A DAY AT THE DORM CAFETERIA TO GET YOUR RDA OF THE 4 LESSER-KNOWN SUB FOOD GROUPS:

1. THE CHAR & GRISSLE GROUP

2. THE DEEP-FRIED GREASE GROUP

3. THE COLA, 7-UP AND ORANGE-DRINK GROUP

4. THE JELLO GROUP

BUILD A CLOSE RELATIONSHIP WITH YOUR DORM ROOMMATE BY SHOWING HIM YOUR ANUS WHENEVER HE'S IN THE ROOM

CUT IT OUT!

ENDEAR YOURSELF TO YOUR CLASSMATES AND PROFESSORS ALIKE — BRING BEER FOR EVERYONE IN CLASS EVERY DAY

PUBLICLY SUCCUMB TO A CAMPUS STREET PREACHER AND BECOME A MANIACAL CHRISTIAN... THEN TRY TO CONVERT EVERYONE YOU MEET FROM THEN ON

MAY I HELP YOU?

DO YOU KNOW JESUS?

TAKE ALL THE MONEY YOUR PARENTS GIVE YOU FOR SCHOOL AND BET IT ON THE DOG RACES... USE YOUR WINNINGS TO LIVE A LIFE OF LUXURY.

FEELIN' DOWN?

HERE ARE SOME QUICK CHEER-UP TIPS

RENT ANY MOVIE THAT USA TODAY HAS CALLED "THE FEEL-GOOD MOVIE OF THE YEAR!"

TO GET YOU STARTED...

SHORT CIRCUIT
THE KARATE KID II
E. T.
SPACE CAMP
HARRY AND THE HENDERSONS

HARRY! HARRY! COME BACK! WE'RE SORRY!

WATCH THE LOCAL NEWS

OKAY, DANA, I HOPE THINGS WARM UP BY THE WEEKEND! GOODNIGHT, EVERYBODY! AND THANKS FOR WATCHING WISC NEWS-3 — FOR KIDS' SAKE!

BUY "THE BEST OF ERMA BOMBECK" AND READ IT COVER TO COVER

I'LL TELL YA, KIDS'LL DO THE DUMBEST THINGS, BUTCHYA GOTTA LOVE 'EM!

AIR JAM TO THE LATEST CD OF YOUR FAVORITE CHRISTIAN ROCK BAND

BY THE LIGHT OF THE LORD, THE LIGHT OF THE LORD, THE SON IS COMIN'

HE'S COMIN' HE'S COMIN'

LH

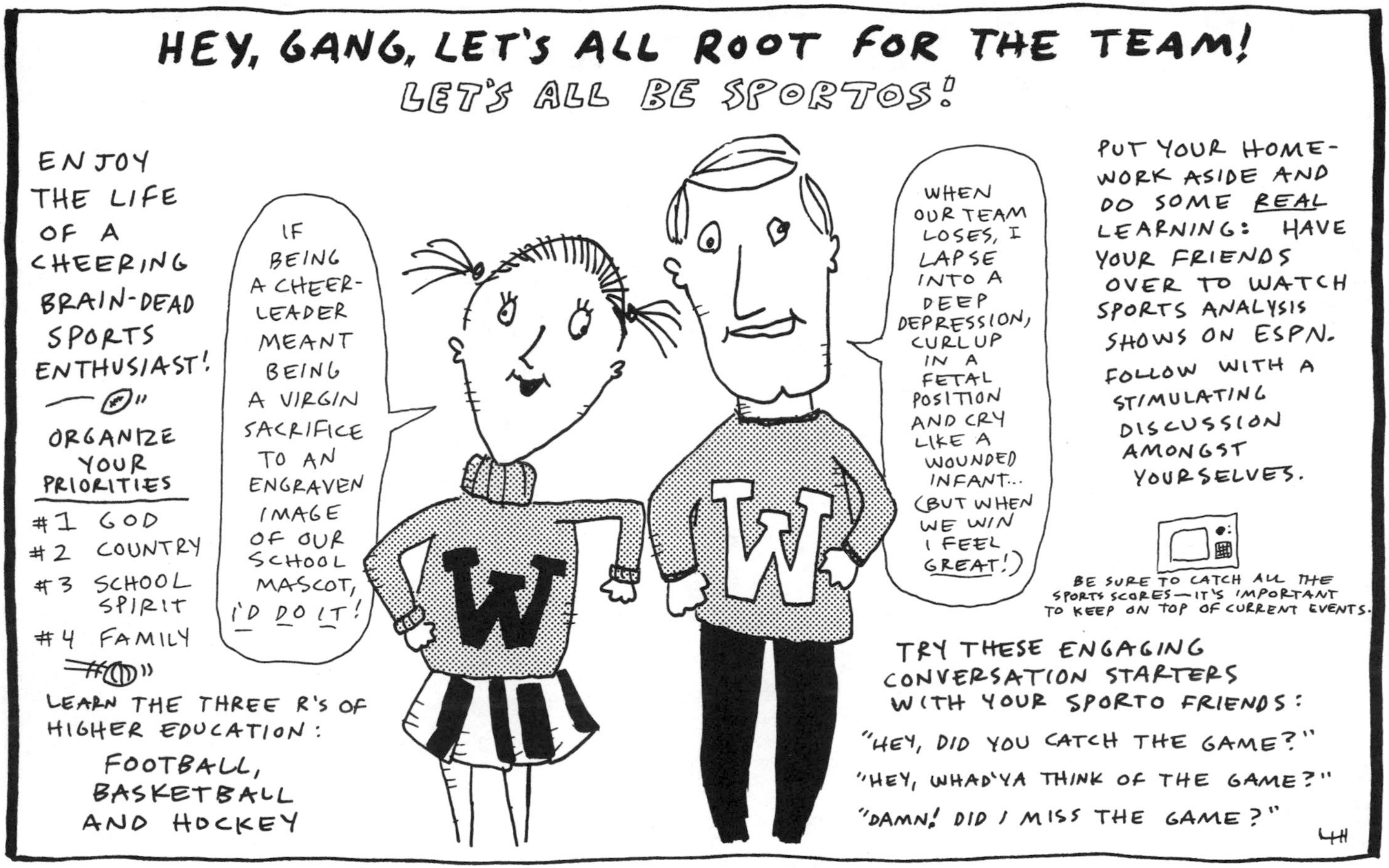
HEY, GANG, LET'S ALL ROOT FOR THE TEAM!
LET'S ALL BE SPORTOS!
ENJOY THE LIFE OF A CHEERING BRAIN-DEAD SPORTS ENTHUSIAST!
ORGANIZE YOUR PRIORITIES
#1 GOD
#2 COUNTRY
#3 SCHOOL SPIRIT
#4 FAMILY
LEARN THE THREE R'S OF HIGHER EDUCATION: FOOTBALL, BASKETBALL AND HOCKEY
IF BEING A CHEERLEADER MEANT BEING A VIRGIN SACRIFICE TO AN ENGRAVEN IMAGE OF OUR SCHOOL MASCOT, I'D DO IT!
WHEN OUR TEAM LOSES, I LAPSE INTO A DEEP DEPRESSION, CURL UP IN A FETAL POSITION AND CRY LIKE A WOUNDED INFANT... (BUT WHEN WE WIN I FEEL GREAT!)
PUT YOUR HOMEWORK ASIDE AND DO SOME REAL LEARNING: HAVE YOUR FRIENDS OVER TO WATCH SPORTS ANALYSIS SHOWS ON ESPN. FOLLOW WITH A STIMULATING DISCUSSION AMONGST YOURSELVES.
BE SURE TO CATCH ALL THE SPORTS SCORES—IT'S IMPORTANT TO KEEP ON TOP OF CURRENT EVENTS.
TRY THESE ENGAGING CONVERSATION STARTERS WITH YOUR SPORTO FRIENDS:
"HEY, DID YOU CATCH THE GAME?"
"HEY, WHAD'YA THINK OF THE GAME?"
"DAMN! DID I MISS THE GAME?"

BE A DIAMOND THIEF!

JUS' LIKE LASSITER!

BE A DEBONAIR PLAYBOY BY DAY, AND A CUNNING BURGLAR BY NIGHT.

LOOK 'IT ALL THE JEWELS ON YOUR NECK! I'M DEF'NATELY ROBBIN' YOU!

YOU'LL BREAK INTO RICH WOMEN'S CASTLES, STEALING THEIR JEWELS — AND THEIR HEARTS.

I LOVE DANGEROUS MEN

SCRAM, YA HAG!

THIS SOUNDS LIKE THE ULTIMATE FANTASY!!

FURTHERMORE, YOUR DORM BUDDIES WILL BE BLOWN-OVER IMPRESSED BY YOUR NEWFOUND CRIMINAL HOBBY.

CHECK IT OUT, DUDES!

WOW! THEY'RE LOVELY!

AND YOU'LL BE RICH BEYOND YOUR DREAMS!

GIMME TWO HELPINGS O' THAT HASH!

DOGGONE YOU, PLEBES! YOU NEVER TOLD ME THE DORM CAFETERIA WOULDN'T ACCEPT RUBIES!!

BUILD YOUR OWN ORGANIZED CRIME RING

START SMALL... MAKE THE SCRAWNIEST, WIMPIEST KIDS IN YOUR DORM PAY YOU A "PROTECTION FEE" TO INSURE THAT YOU WON'T BEAT THEM UP.

CAN I PLEASE JUST HAVE ONE MORE WEEK TO RAISE THE MONEY?

A WHOLE WEEK, HUH? GEE, Y'KNOW IT'D BE A SHAME IF DURING THAT WEEK YOU WERE TO FALL IN THE SHOWER AND BREAK YOUR LEG, OR TRIP ON THE STAIRS AND CRACK OPEN YOUR SKULL...

WITH THE MONEY YOU MAKE, HIRE TWO OR THREE OF THE BIGGEST KIDS IN YOUR DORM TO GET PROTECTION MONEY FROM EVERYBODY.

CAN I JUST HAVE ONE MORE WEEK? I PROMISE I'LL HAVE THE MONEY IN ONE WEEK!

ROCKO, DIS FELLA DON'T SEEM TA WANNA LIFT A FINGER TA HELP US OUT. MAYBE WE OUGHTA HELP HIM TA LIFT A FINGER— GRAB HIS ARM!

WITH ALL THE MONEY YOU EARN, FINANCE GAMBLING, DRINKING, AND WEAPONS-PURCHASING OPPORTUNITIES FOR YOUR CLASSMATES

YOU'LL MAKE A FORTUNE!

HEY, WAIT A MINUTE, PLEBES... WHAT AM I GETTING INTO? ISN'T THIS WRONG? COULDN'T I GO TO PRISON FOR A LONG TIME IF I'M CAUGHT DOING ALL THIS?

THAT LEADS TO THE NEXT STEP: PAY THE POLICE TO KEEP THEIR NOSE OUT OF YOUR AFFAIRS... IF ANY OFFICER REFUSES TO ACCEPT PAY, TERRORIZE HIS FAMILY WITH YOUR TEAM OF THUGS!

WHEW! I WAS GETTING A LITTLE WORRIED THERE FOR A SECOND!

YOU'LL LIVE YOUR LIFE WITHOUT THE PETTY RESTRICTIONS IMPOSED BY THE LAW...

IF SOMEBODY BORROWS YOUR FAVORITE CD AND FAILS TO RETURN IT WITHIN A REASONABLE TIME— KILL HIM!

RATTA TATTA TATTA TAT

IF YOUR ROOMMATE FAILS TO PICKUP HIS SIDE OF THE ROOM TO YOUR SATISFACTION— KILL HIM!

FFPT!

IF A PROFESSOR GIVES YOU AN F— KILL HIM!

PTEW!

YOU'LL GET EVERYTHING YOU WANT BY INSPIRING FEAR AND RESPECT IN EVERYONE.

MOM, DAD, MY MONTHLY ALLOWANCE IS OVERDUE... BRUNO, WHY DON'T YOU AND THE BOYS TAKE MOM & DAD FOR A LITTLE DRIVE IN THE COUNTRY

TIRED OF ALWAYS WITNESSING VIOLENT CRIMES AND FEELING POWERLESS TO INTERVENE?	TIRED OF OVERHEARING SUPERVILLAINS' PLANS TO RULE THE WORLD AND FEELING HELPLESS TO DO ANYTHING ABOUT IT?

THEN BECOME A SUPERHERO!

IT'S EASIER THAN YOU MIGHT THINK!

FIRST, YOU MUST GET SUPER-HUMAN POWERS. IT'S EASY

HANG AROUND IN SCIENTIFIC LABORATORIES A LOT AND HOPE YOU'RE INVOLVED IN A SERIOUS ACCIDENT

IF YOU WANT...	THEN ALL YOU HAVE TO DO IS...	AND DON'T WORRY, THERE'S VERY LITTLE CHANCE THAT...
SUPER STRENGTH / X-RAY VISION	MISTAKENLY GET INJECTED WITH A SUPER-STRENGTH SERUM DEVELOPED BY GOVERNMENT SCIENTISTS TO CREATE THE PERFECT SOLDIER.	THE SERUM WILL CAUSE PSYCHOLOGICAL DAMAGE, RELEGATING YOU TO A LIFE OF UNCONTROLLABLE MUSCLE SPASMS AND DROOLING.
TO FLY AS FAST AS A ROCKETSHIP	ACCIDENTALLY DOUSE YOUR EYES WITH A SPECIAL GENE-ALTERING ACID DESIGNED FOR A MIRACLE CARROT-GROWTH PRODUCT.	YOUR EYES WILL DISSOLVE INTO A BLOODY PULP, LEAVING YOU PERMANENTLY BLIND AND DISFIGURED.
TO HAVE THE 6TH SENSE AND DEXTEROUS CUNNING OF NATURE'S MOST DANGEROUS CREATURES.	BE IN AN ELECTRONICS LAB WHEN IT GETS STRUCK BY LIGHTNING.	YOU'LL GO UP IN FLAMES AND DIE SCREAMING LIKE A LUNATIC.
	ACCIDENTALLY GET BITTEN BY A RADIOACTIVE GOPHER SNAKE.	THE BITE WILL BECOME INFECTED AND YOU'LL DIE.

FINALLY, DESIGN AN ATTRACTIVE COSTUME AND DECIDE HOW YOU'LL USE YOUR POWERS TO MAKE THE WORLD A BETTER PLACE TO LIVE...

DALE™ THE DRUNKEN COLLEGE-STUDENT DOLL

HIS OBNOXIOUS BESOTTED ANTICS WILL GIVE YOU HOURS OF PLAYTIME FUN!

NEW FROM MATEL®

HEAR HIM SAY:

- RUB HIM AND HE URINATES!
- SQUEEZE HIM AND HE VOMITS!

(COMES WITH REFILLABLE BEER CAN)

- SIMPLE ONE-SNAP PANTS FOR EASY MOONING!
- LOPSIDED FEET SO HE CAN'T STAND UP!

DUDE! I GOT A EXAM TOMORROW!

OH, NO WAY! SHIT! THIS IS, LIKE, MY BEST SHIRT!

♪ JUMPIN' JACK FLASH EH EH EH-EH EHH... ♪♪

OW, OW, OWOOOOOO!!

AND MORE LAUGHING, HOWLING, OUT-OF-TUNE SINGING, AND UNINTELLIGIBLE BABBLING!

ONLY $19.95

PLAYACT **DRUNKEN DALE'S**™ BAR-TIME REVELRY WITH HIS BUDDIES, **INEBRIATED NEIL**™ AND **PLASTERED PETE**™ (SOLD SEPARATELY)...

PRETEND THE BAR'S JUST CLOSED, AND DALE'S LOOKIN' FOR MORE GOOD TIMES...

IMAGINE HIS CHARMING BREATH AND UNENGAGED SPEECH AS HE LURES **CAROUSING COED KATE**™ (ALSO FROM MATEL) BACK TO HIS DORM ROOM...

PRETEND HE'S A LOSER IN BED DESPITE HIS HEFTY STASH OF CONDOMS!

LTH!

EARN BIG BUCKS WITH DIGNITY
WITH PLEBES'
EASY GET-RICH-QUICK SCHEMES

BE A PRINTMAKER

MODERN SILK-SCREEN AND CHROMALIN PRINTING TECHNOLOGIES HAVE PUT THE FUN BACK INTO COUNTERFEITING. PASSÉ, YOU SAY? TOO OBVIOUS? THAT'S PRECISELY WHY NO ONE WILL EVER SUSPECT YOU! NOBODY LOOKS CLOSELY AT CRUMPLED $20 BILLS.

BECOME A SUCCESSFUL MERCHANT

VISIT A NEIGHBORHOOD BUILDING CONSTRUCTION SITE LATE AT NIGHT AND TAKE AS MANY DOORS, PIPES OR SHEETS OF PLASTER AS YOU CAN. THEN SELL THEM WHOLESALE TO A NEARBY BUILDING SUPPLY STORE.

SERVE THE LORD

BECOME THE PASTOR OF A LOCAL CHURCH AND KEEP EVERY LAST CENT FROM THE SUNDAY COLLECTION PLATES FOR YOURSELF. WHO'S GOING TO THINK THE <u>PASTOR</u> WOULD STEAL?

HEY, LOOK AT ME! I'M A POET!

BE A POET LAUREATE

WRITE AN ELABORATE GRANT PROPOSAL TO THE NATIONAL ENDOWMENT FOR THE ARTS TO WRITE POETRY—AND SPEND ALL THE MONEY ON BEER!

LH

"PLEBES" TORTURE SURVIVAL TECHNIQUES

YOU'VE JUST BEEN CAPTURED BY A HOSTILE FOREIGN POWER, AND THEY PLAN TO TORTURE YOU TO EXTRACT MILITARY SECRETS.

BUT I DON'T KNOW NUTHIN'!

BUT, SEE, THEY DON'T KNOW THAT!

YOUR "PLEBES" TORTURE SURVIVAL TECHNIQUES COME INTO PLAY AS SOON AS THEY STRAP YOU ONTO THEIR TORTURE TABLE.

CAN'T WE DO A "PLEBES" THIS WEEK ABOUT SUMMER BEACH FUN?

FIRST, CONVINCE YOURSELF THAT PAIN IS ONLY YOUR BODY'S WAY OF COMMUNICATING TO YOUR BRAIN WHAT IT'S GOING THROUGH— IT'S NOT REAL

SO, THEY'RE NOT REALLY SHOOTING HOT LEAD UP MY ASS?

NEXT, IMAGINE A PLEASANT MEMORY.

AT MY REALLY FUN TENTH BIRTHDAY PARTY, I HAD A COCONUT-LEMON BIRTHDAY CAKE THAT, COME TO THINK OF IT, WAS SHAPED LIKE HOT LEAD BEING SHOT UP SOMEBODY'S ASS

FINALLY, AFTER YOU'VE BEEN RELEASED, FOCUS ON THE FUTURE, NOT THE PAST.

SOME FUTURE... I'LL NEVER BE ABLE TO TAKE ANOTHER CRAP AS LONG AS I LIVE!!

YOU CAN BE SOMEBODY!

BUT I'M A NOBODY— JUST AN AVERAGE SIMPLETON WITH NO SPECIAL TALENTS OR SKILLS

YOU'RE AN AVERAGE SIMPLETON BECAUSE THAT'S WHAT YOU'VE MADE OF YOURSELF

YOU CAN JUST AS EASILY MAKE YOURSELF INTO A TRUELY IMPRESSIVE HUMAN BEING.

FIRST, BUY SOME FANCY CLOTHES. THIS WILL IMMEDIATELY SET YOU APART FROM THE REST OF THE PACK

HEY—I ALREADY FEEL LIKE SOMEBODY!

NEXT—ALTER THE WAY YOU SPEAK TO SOUND LIKE SOMEONE CONFIDENT AND POWERFUL· TRY ORSON WELLES OR THURSTEN HOWELL, III.

USE YOUR NEW VOICE WHEREVER YOU GO.

I SAY, CHUCK, MY GOOD MAN, ARE YOU GOING TO EAT ALL YOUR FRIES?

STEP 3— DUMP ALL YOUR OLD FRIENDS. YOU'RE NOW FAR SUPERIOR TO THEM AND THEY ONLY DRAG YOU DOWN.

BEFRIEND NEW, IMPORTANT PEOPLE: BANKERS, POLITICIANS, GREAT ARTISTS AND THINKERS. YOU'LL FIT RIGHT IN

THAT'S A AWESOME — TIE, SIR!

THEN FIND A CAUSE AND STICK TO IT TILL YOU GET MEDIA ATTENTION.

JAPANESE ECONOMIC SUPREMACY

MUSIC CENSORSHIP

THE RAPIDLY SINKING QUALITY OF FROZEN PIZZA BURGERS

OR ANYTHING THAT RATTLES YOUR NOGGIN

FINALLY, START EXPRESSING YOUR OPINION ABOUT CURRENT EVENTS. NEWSPAPERS WILL QUOTE YOU. TV WILL INTERVIEW YOU...

Wall St. Journal
DARREN SAYS FUTURES PRICES WILL STABILIZE

SWIMWEAR WEEKLY
DARREN'S PICKS FOR HOTTEST BIKINIS OF THE DECADE!

TED, I THINK THE HOUSE JUDICIARY COMMITTEE IS BASICALLY A BUNCHA PRICKS...

NIGHTLINE

PRETTY SOON YOU'LL BE ADVISING PRESIDENTS! ENDORSING MAJOR BREAKAST CEREALS! HOSTING YOUR OWN CABLE ACCESS TV SHOW!

AND ALL IT TAKES IS A LITTLE CONFIDENCE IN YOURSELF.

I CAN BE SOMEBODY! I CAN!

MAKE YOUR OWN ADOLESCENT PARTY MOVIE

CONNECT SCENES FROM EACH COLUMN, LEFT TO RIGHT, AND CREATE UP TO 1024 POSSIBLE R-RATED PLOTS FOR YOUR OWN TEENAGE TITTY FLICKS!

THE SET-UP	THE BUMMER	THE COME-BACK	THE PEEP	THE RESOLUTION
3 BUDDIES MAKE A BET THAT THEY CAN SEDUCE THE HEAD CHEERLEADER	ONE BUDDY'S DAD GROUNDS HIM FOR 2 WEEKS	THE 3 BUDDIES GET JOBS AT JAKE'S LOTTA BURGER AND EARN $500 BY FRIDAY	THE BUDDIES GET A PEEK AT THE CHEERLEADERS IN THE SHOWER	ALL 3 BUDDIES GET LAID, AND THE SCHOOL JOCK FALLS IN THE SEPTIC TANK
3 BUDDIES FIND OUT ONE OF THEIR AUNTS DIED AND LEFT THEM A MANSION IN BEVERLY HILLS	A PENCIL-NECKED TEACHER SENTENCES ONE BUDDY TO TEN DAYS AFTER SCHOOL CLEANING CHALKBOARDS	THE 3 BUDDIES DRESS UP AS AN ALLIGATOR, A PIRATE AND A GORILLA, AND SPIKE THE PUNCH AT THE SCHOOL COSTUME PARTY	THE BUDDIES CLIMB A LADDER AND LOOK IN THE HEAD CHEERLEADER'S DORM WINDOW WHILE SHE'S UNDRESSING	ALL 3 BUDDIES GET LAID, AND THE SCHOOL JOCK GETS DOUSED WITH 8 TONS OF TARTAR SAUCE
3 BUDDIES HAVE A ONCE-IN-A-LIFETIME CHANCE TO GO TO FLORIDA FOR SPRING BREAK	ONE BUDDY ACCIDENTALLY DRIVES THE SCHOOL JOCK'S EXPENSIVE SPORTS CAR INTO A PIT OF WET CEMENT	THE 3 BUDDIES ORDER A STRIP-O-GRAM FOR THE COLLEGE DEAN.	ONE BUDDY SPILLS WHIPPED CREAM ON THE HEAD CHEERLEADER'S SHIRT, AND TALKS HER INTO TAKING IT OFF SO HE CAN CLEAN IT	ALL 3 BUDDIES GET LAID—AND ONE OF THEIR CATCH IS THE SCHOOL JOCK'S GIRLFRIEND
3 BUDDIES FIND OUT ONE MEMBER OF THEIR GANG HAS NEVER GOTTEN LAID	THE 3 BUDDIES ARE PELTED WITH PEE-FILLED BALLOONS BY THE SCHOOL JOCK AND HIS TEAMMATES.	2 OF THE BUDDIES TELL THE HEAD CHEERLEADER THAT THE OTHER BUDDY'S GIRLFRIEND JUST DIED, AND HE NEEDS CONSOLATION	THE BUDDIES VISIT A HOOKER, WHO COMES ON SO STRONG THAT THEY RUN AWAY IN FEAR	ALL 3 BUDDIES GET LAID, AND THE SCHOOL JOCK IS LOCKED IN A CLOSET WITH THE UGLIEST GIRL IN SCHOOL

LH

BECOME A MASTER OF
HYPNOSIS
CONTROL THE WORLD BY TAPPING INTO UNSUSPECTING VICTIMS' SUB-CONSCIOUS MINDS — ALL YOU NEED IS A GOLD WATCH!
YOU ARE GETTING VERRRY SLEEEPY
IT WORKS!
NOW TRY PLANTING SOME SIMPLE POST-HYPNOTIC SUGGES-TIONS.
YOU WILL BE MY SLAVE
YES... MAS... TER...
I CAN'T BE STOPPED!
YOU WILL PROTECT AND SERVE ONLY ME!
YOU WILL BE MY WIFE!
YOU WILL WASH MY FEET!
THIS IS AWESOME! I'M THE MASTER OF THE WORLD!
BRING ME MORE PIZZAS, YOU APES!
CLINK
OH NO! MY WATCH!
WE'RE GONNA BEAT THE CRAP OUTTA YOU!
HELP, PLEBES!

MAKE OFF LIKE A BANDIT WITH
THE PLEBES TEXTBOOK SCAM

STEP 1
GET A DEGREE AND BECOME A PROFESSOR

STEP 2
WRITE A TEXTBOOK IN YOUR CHOSEN FIELD, BORROWING HEAVILY FROM OTHER BOOKS (USE FOOTNOTES)

ANCIENT INUIT LANGUAGE DEVELOPMENT 3000-1300 B.C. BY SHAUN "THE CHUGMASTER" MULHEREN

STEP 3
SELL YOUR TEXTBOOK TO COLLEGE BOOKSTORES AT AN ABSURD MARK-UP

LESSEE, IT COST $2 TO PRINT EACH BOOK... A $168 COVER PRICE SOUNDS FAIR!

STEP 4
CALL YOUR COLLEGE BOOKSTORE AND PLACE AN ORDER FOR YOUR BOOK TO USE IN YOUR CLASS

YEAH— I GOTTA ORDER 80 OF THIS ONE CERTAIN BOOK... AND BILL THE UNIVERSITY!

THAT SIMPLE CALL MADE YOU SEVERAL THOUSAND DOLLARS! AND THAT'S JUST YOUR CLASS — THINK OF THE DOZENS OF OTHER PROFESSORS WHO WILL ORDER YOUR BOOK!

DOZENS? LEMME GET MY CALCULATOR!

STEP 5
NOW, EVERY SEMESTER, SWITCH A FEW PARAGRAPHS AROUND AND CALL IT A NEW EDITION! LIKE YOU, PROFESSORS WILL HAVE TO KEEP BUYING YOUR BOOK YEAR AFTER YEAR, SO THEIR STUDENTS CAN FOLLOW ALONG ON THE RIGHT PAGES!

BUT WAIT— IT TURNS OUT A PROFESSOR IN PEEDUNK, IOWA, IS SELLING HIS STUDENTS XEROXED COPIES OF YOUR FIRST EDITION EACH YEAR!

OH NO! HOW MUCH WOULD I LOSE ON THAT?

YOU DON'T LOSE — YOU GAIN! FIND OUT THE XEROX SHOP THAT MADE THE COPIES AND SUE THEIR PANTS OFF FOR COPYRIGHT INFRINGEMENT! GET HUNDREDS OF THOUSANDS OF DOLLARS!

THIS IS GREAT! AND I NEVER USED TO LIKE MATH!

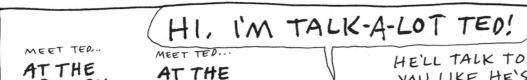

HI, I'M TALK-A-LOT TED!

MEET TED...
AT THE GROCERY STORE

IS THAT SMUCKERS JAM? MM, MM! "IF IT'S SMUCKERS, IT HAS TO BE GOOD!" HA HA HA! HOW LONG YOU BEEN WAITING? I COME HERE A LOT. THIS EXPRESS LANE IS PRIT-TEE SLOW, HUH?

MEET TED...
AT THE LAUNDROMAT

IS THIS HOW YOU FOLD SHIRTS? I CAN NEVER DO IT VERY WELL. HOW IS LIQUID TIDE? I'VE NEVER TRIED IT. THIS IS A GREAT PLACE TO MEET PEOPLE. HEY, LET'S DO OUR WASH TOGETHER NEXT TIME!

HE'LL TALK TO YOU LIKE HE'S KNOWN YOU FOR YEARS WHETHER YOU LIKE IT OR NOT — HE CAN'T TELL!

LOOK FOR

- BAD BREATH
- CLAMMY HANDS
- ABYSMAL SENSE OF HUMOR
- UNDERDEVELOPED SEX ORGANS
- A STRANGE TWITCH IN ONE EYE THAT YOU CAN'T HELP STARING AT.

MEET TED...
ON THE BUS

I DIDN'T USED TO TAKE THIS BUS. IT WAS THE DOWNTOWN E WHEN I USED TO RIDE IT. HOWABOUT THE CROSSTOWN J? YOU EVER RIDE THE CROSSTOWN J? WHATCHYA READIN'?

HE LOVES THE BARBER

SO, ARE YOU IN SCHOOL?

YEAH, I'M TAKING 3 CLASSES. I'M LEARNING A LOT OF THINGS. SAY, WHERE DID YOU LEARN TO CUT HAIR?

I WENT TO SCHOOL FOR IT. I LIKE SCHOOL. DON'T YOU? LET'S TALK ABOUT IT.

OH YES! YES!!

LH

DO YOU HAVE WHAT IT TAKES TO WORK AT THE CAMPUS RADIO STATION?

CAN YOU...

... NERVOUSLY MUMBLE YOUR WAY THROUGH IMPROMPTU CHITCHAT?

... CUE UP RECORDS ON THE AIR WHILE ANOTHER RECORD IS PLAYING?

... FORGET TO TURN OFF YOUR MICROPHONE AND ACCIDENTALLY SAY, "GOD, I WANNA GET OUTTA HERE SO I CAN GO TAKE A CRAP" ON THE AIR?

HELLO, MY NAME IS BRBL, I MEAN BRIAN, BRIAN BLINT, UM, A-AND HERE'S A RECORD, IT'S THE NITTY GRITTY DIRT BAND I THINK. I GUESS. IT'S A COOL RECORD.

GAIN VALUABLE EXPERIENCE...

... TRYING TO SOUND CALM!

... BEGGING YOUR FRIENDS NOT TO TUNE IN AND LISTEN TO YOU!

... PANICKING WHILE WONDERING WHAT TO DO DURING A TWO-MINUTE SPELL OF DEAD AIR!

IF YOU MEET THE CRITERIA, YOU COULD VERY WELL HAVE YOUR VOICE BROADCAST FROM A <u>40-WATT</u> TRANSMITTER ACROSS ALMOST THE <u>WHOLE CAMP</u>US, WITH A POTENTIAL LISTENING AUDIENCE OF S<u>EVERA</u>L PEOPLE!

THE "PLEBES" GUIDE TO COOL
COOL
NOT COOL
COOL
NOT COOL
COOL
NOT COOL
PLAYBOY
SHE-MALE MONTHLY
TROTAN
MACE
COOL
NOT COOL
COOL
NOT COOL
COOL
NOT COOL
MILLER BEER
GINSENG ROOT BEER
AWESOME!
SPLENDID!
COOL
NOT COOL
COOL
NOT COOL
COOL
NOT COOL
OH, TODD, HONEY!
OH, TODD, HONEY!
STOP

PRESIDENT OF THE UNITED STATES

THE NEXT ELECTION WILL BE HERE BEFORE YOU KNOW IT— START YOUR CAMPAIGN NOW!

ALL YOU NEED IS 3 THINGS:

1 ENORMOUS WEALTH

YOU'VE ALREADY SUCCESSFULLY COMPLETED PLEBES' "ROAD TO FINANCIAL NIRVANA" PROGRAM, SO YOU SHOULD HAVE ALL THE MONEY YOU NEED.

2 A SPOUSE AND NO LESS THAN 3 CHILDREN

WITH A SPOOKY, TEXTBOOK-DRAFTED, "NORMAL" NUCLEAR FAMILY, YOU WILL BE ACCEPTED BY VOTERS AS A DEVOTED LEADER, AS OPPOSED TO A MEMBER OF A MYSTERIOUS FRINGE GROUP.

3 A GOOD SUIT

NO ONE WILL TAKE YOU SERIOUSLY AS A CANDIDATE FOR PRESIDENT UNLESS YOU'RE ALWAYS WEARING A GOOD SUIT.

NOW CHOOSE ONE OF THE MAJOR POLITICAL PARTIES— IT MAKES NO DIFFERENCE WHICH

MEMORIZE THIS SIMPLE VOTE-SNATCHING POLITICAL PLATFORM:

① PEACE, PROSPERITY AND EDUCATION

② FAMILY, FREEDOM, AND THE AMERICAN FLAG

③ NO TAXES ANYMORE—EVER!

MEMORIZE THESE CROWD-PLEASING INSTANT-WIN SLOGANS:

① "I'M PROUD TO BE A CITIZEN OF THE UNITED STATES OF AMERICA!"

② "ON JANUARY 20TH, NINETEEN-HUNDRED AND NINETY-THREE, I WILL BE THE NEXT PRESIDENT OF THE UNITED STATES OF AMERICA!"

③ "GOD BLESS THE UNITED STATES OF AMERICA!"

RULE OF THUMB: AMERICAN VOTERS ARE STONE DUMB— KEEP THINGS SIMPLE!

CHOOSE YOUR RUNNING MATE CAREFULLY

LINDA HERE IS A PART-BLACK, PART-HISPANIC, PART-CHEROKEE INDIAN WOMAN FROM TEXAS— WITH HER I'LL ACE THE SOUTH IN THE PRIMARY, I'LL HAVE THE MINORITY VOTE, THE WOMEN'S VOTE...

AND SHE'S DUMB AS A POST AND SHORTER THAN ME—SO IT'LL STILL LOOK LIKE I'M IN CHARGE!

NOW YOU'RE THINKING LIKE A PRESIDENT!

NOW COMES THE IMPORTANT PART: SPENDING MONEY. YOU NEED TO BUY TV ADS TILL YOUR FACE IS AS RECOGNIZABLE AS RONALD MCDONALD

MAKE USE OF ALL THOSE PHRASES YOU LEARNED

GOD BLESS AMERICA!

NO MORE TAXES!

PEACE, PROSPERITY!

FAMILY, FREEDOM!

AND SURE ENOUGH, YOU'LL BE PRESIDENT OF THE UNITED STATES!

PARTY!!

THE SECRET LIFE
OF BILL TIDBAUM, SOPHOMORE

EVERY ONCE IN A WHILE, AFTER HIS ROOMMATE'S GONE TO SLEEP, HE GRABS THE VASELINE INTENSIVE CARE LOTION AND SLINKS OFF TO THE 25¢ PEEP SHOW.

WHILE STUDYING AT THE LIBRARY, HE DAYDREAMS OF ONE DAY BEATING UP HIS HIGH SCHOOL BULLY, UTILIZING THE SKILLS HE LEARNED WATCHING EVERY EPISODE OF "KUNG FU."

WHEN HE'S HOME ALONE, HE PERFORMS A CHIPPENDALE DANCER STRIPTEASE ACT IN FRONT OF THE MIRROR.

HIS FRIENDS KNOW HIM AS A HAPPY-GO-LUCKY PARTYIN' BONANZA, BUT IN PRIVATE, HE SITS IN HIS ROOM AND WATCHES "EIGHT IS ENOUGH," SOMETIMES SHEDDING A TEAR DURING THE LAST SCENE, LONGING TO TELL HIS MOM AND DAD HOW MUCH HE MISSES HOME.

THOUGH KNOWN AS A SKEPTIC AMONG HIS DORM BUDDIES, HE GETS DOWN ON HIS KNEES EVERY NIGHT AND PRAYS SO HARD HE SWEATS, BEGGING GOD TO GET HIM LAID BEFORE HE'S 20.

LH

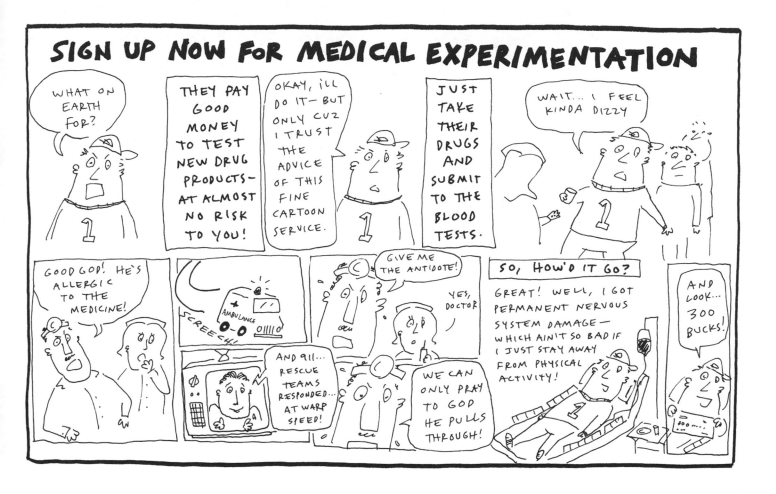

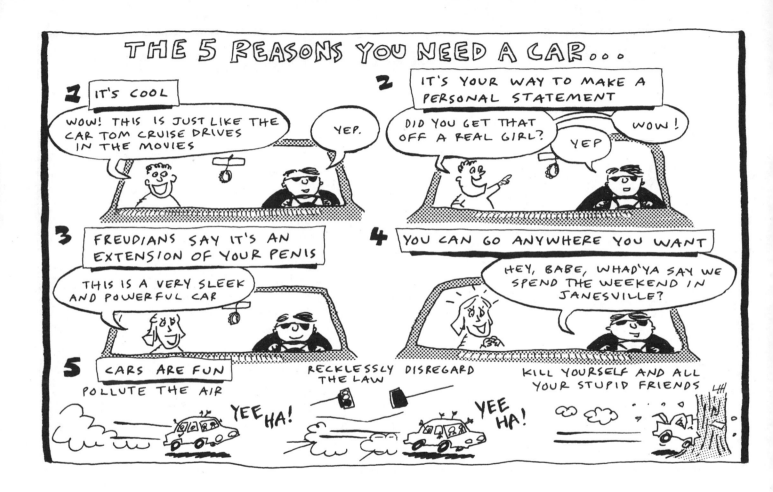

PLEBES ON TWO WHEELS

THE OFFICIAL "PLEBES" BICYCLE OPERATOR'S MANUAL

SAFETY TIPS

- SUDDEN, ERRATIC MOVEMENTS MAKE YOU HARD TO HIT

- BE CAREFREE— IT'S PEDESTRIANS AND MOTORISTS' JOB TO LOOK OUT FOR YOU!

TRY THESE FUN GAMES

- GREG LeMOND DOES BUSINESS-DISTRICT SIDEWALK

- ALL COLORS ARE GREEN

RULES OF THUMB

- HAND TURN SIGNALS ARE FOR SISSIES

- HELMETS ARE FOR SISSIES UNDER 12

- PEDESTRIANS ARE JUST PYLONS IN MOTION

HONK HONK HONK

WHY'S THAT GUY HONKIN' AT ME? I DON'T RECOGNIZE HIM, BUT I'LL WAVE BACK ANYWAY

TURN YOUR EVERYDAY EXPERIENCES INTO A...

BEST-SELLING NOVEL

THE FIRST RULE OF WRITING IS "WRITE WHAT YOU KNOW." THAT MEANS YOU CAN MAKE A ZILLION DOLLARS—JUST LIKE STEPHEN KING OR JACKIE COLLINS—WRITING ABOUT YOUR EVERYDAY EXPERIENCES... IN ANY GENRE!

ROMANCE

DECEMBER
THE NEW MONTH ON MY CINDY CRAWFORD CALENDAR

EXPOSÉ

DORM FOOD SUCKS

MYSTERY

WHY DO I KEEP GETTING THESE DAMNED ZITS?!
?

SCIENCE FICTION

IT'S ALMOST LIKE IT'S
IT'S ALIVE!
THE DORM-ROOM MINI-FRIDGE THAT KEEPS BREAKING DOWN

CRIME

CHECK IT OUT— I SWIPED THIS HIGHWAY THING!

HORROR

MY ROOMMATE LEFT HIS DIRTY UNDERWEAR LYING AROUND AND THERE WERE STAINS ON IT!

BIOGRAPHY

TOO MUCH FOOD
THE SHORT LIFE AND FAST TIMES OF MELVIN THE GOLDFISH

HUMOR

I'M OVER THE HILL! I JUST TURNED 20!

FINAL EXAM

1. BULLSHIT YOUR WAY THROUGH A VAGUE SUMMARY OF THE IDEAS COVERED IN THIS COURSE. INCLUDE SEVERAL MISSPELLINGS AND GRAMMATICAL ERRORS.

2. YOU'VE WATCHED ME LECTURE FOR 16 WEEKS. LIST SOME OF MY ODD QUIRKS, GESTURES AND REPEATED PHRASES THAT HAVE ANNOYED AND AMUSED YOU.

3. DESCRIBE IN DETAIL YOUR MOST ROLLICKING DRUNKEN STUPOR OF THE SEMESTER. CITE EXAMPLES OF YOUR FRIENDS' RECOLLECTIONS TO SUPPORT YOUR THESIS.

OF THE ABOVE 3 QUESTIONS, ANSWER THE ONE YOU CAN BEST FAKE YOUR WAY THROUGH, RANSACKING YOUR GENERAL KNOWLEDGE AND PEEKING AT ANY NOTES YOU MAY HAVE UNDER YOUR DESK OR WRITTEN ON YOUR HAND.

LH

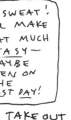

GETTING ALONG WITH COMMONERS

A PLEBES SOCIAL-SERVICE GUIDE

YOU'RE A MEMBER OF THE INTELLIGENTSIA—SOPHISTICATED AND COLLEGE EDUCATED. SO HOW CAN YOU RELATE MEANINGFULLY WITH THOSE IN THE LOWER ORDERS? NO PROBLEM! JUST MEMORIZE THESE SIMPLE PHRASES AND CUT THROUGH SOCIAL BARRIERS WITH EASE!

PHRASE	WHEN TO USE IT
"YOU GOT THAT RIGHT" ←	WHEN A DELIVERY-TRUCK DRIVER COMPLAINS TO YOU THAT THE LITTLE GUY IS ALWAYS GETTING SCREWED OVER.
"YEAH—YOU AND ME BOTH" ←	WHEN A FRIEND'S SISTER-IN-LAW TELLS YOU AT A WEDDING RECEPTION THAT SHE NEEDS A VACATION OR SHE'LL LOSE HER MIND.
"I HEAR YA" ←	WHEN A CASHIER AT SHOPCO SAYS IT'S BEEN ONE HECTIC MONDAY.
"YOU SAID IT" ←	WHEN THE WAITRESS AT THE DINER SERVES YOU A CUP OF COFFEE AND SAYS, "NOTHING LIKE BLACK COFFEE TO GET YOUR MOTOR HUMMING."
"AIN'T THAT THE TRUTH" ←	WHEN AN OLD RETIREE TELLS YOU THAT IT'S ABOUT TIME WE GOT SOME DECENT WEATHER.
"DON'T I KNOW IT" ←	WHEN A CAB DRIVER POSITS THAT ALL POLITICIANS ARE CROOKS.
"YOU CAN SAY THAT AGAIN" ←	WHEN YOUR BANK TELLER THANKS GOD IT'S FRIDAY

VISIT A NURSING HOME

SHARPEN YOUR LOCAL NEWS BANTER

YOU'RE THE SPORTS REPORTER ON THE LOCAL EVENING NEWS TEAM.

AND SO, THE PINUITS NEED A BIG WIN OVER THE HUSKERS AT SATURDAY'S GAME... UH...

IT'S TIME TO "PASS THE BALL," SO TO SPEAK, TO THE HEAD ANCHOR. TRY A SIMPLE, "BACK TO YOU, KIP."

UM... HELP ME OUT HERE, KIP, I AIN'T GOT NOTHIN' ELSE TO SAY...

GOOD, BUT NOT GREAT. NOW, BEFORE KIP MOVES ON, HE'LL PROBABLY TRY TO ENGAGE YOU IN A BIT OF BANTER.

WELL, WE LOOK FORWARD TO THAT GAME. AND—WHO KNOWS?—MAYBE KAROWSKI WILL CLINCH THAT STATE RECORD—WHAD'YA THINK?

MAKE IT QUICK—JUST ENOUGH FOR SOME CLOSURE SO KIP CAN MOVE ON TO BETTER THINGS.

UH, WELL... LESSEE...

NO—DON'T LOOK UP THE EXACT RECORD! MAKE SOMETHING UP, QUICK! MAYBE, "YEAH, HE NEEDS 25 MORE COMPLETIONS, AND HE COULD VERY WELL PULL IT OFF." YOU'RE BOTCHING UP THE NEWSCAST PACE!

UH... WAIT—YOU SAID KAROWSKI?

YOU BLEW IT. KIP HAD TO PLOW AHEAD WITHOUT YOU.

UH, COMING UP, A REPORT ON SOME BABY DUCKS AND A NEAR MISS. STAY WITH US.

DARNIT!

LET'S VISIT PREHISTORIC EARTH!

THE "PLEBES" GUIDE TO
CREATING PLASTIC COPINGS FOR DENTAL BRIDGES
HUH?
FIRST, GET A MOLD OF THE DENTAL PATIENT'S TEETH.
I DON'T WANNA BE DOIN' THIS!
NOW HEAT THE COPING PLASTIC UNTIL IT'S PLIABLE.
THIS IS STUPID!
CAREFULLY DRAPE THE PLASTIC OVER THE TOOTH AND CUT IT JUST ABOVE THE GUM LINE.
NO WAY... I QUIT! THIS IS THE WORST PLEBES EVER!
WHY COULDN'T I A'GOT A BILLION DOLLARS OR A AWESOME BABE OR SOMETHIN'!
I'M GOIN' BACK TO MY DORM ROOM!
SHUCKTER HALL
5TH FLOOR
TODD AND GUS'S ROOM
GET OUT!
BUDWEISER
NOW I'M BORED STIFF!

SUMMER SESSION STUDENTS

SULTANS OF LEARNING

THEIR CREDO:
"AN UNENDING STRING OF DEBILITATINGLY DULL TEXTBOOKS IS THE SPICE O' LIFE!"

MY FAVORITE SUMMER-TIME LEISURE ACTIVITY IS READING MY TEXTBOOK WHILE COOPED UP IN A GLOOMY STUDY LIBRARY

I GUESS I'M A LOT MORE RECKLESSLY FUN-LOVING... I SOMETIMES USE A HIGHLIGHTER OR EVEN WRITE NOTES IN THE MARGIN

WHERE DO THEY COME FROM?

AN OBSCURE RELIGIOUS SECT MADE UP OF CLAMMY-SKINNED ANEMICS WHO BELIEVE VACATIONS, BIKING AND BEACH VOLLYBALL ARE THE TOOLS OF SATAN.

A RACE OF MOLE PEOPLE WHO'VE EVOLVED IN DANK SUBTERRANEAN HOLLOWS, UNAWARE OF THE "SURFACE DWELLERS" ABOVE.

WHO ARE THEY?

16-YEAR-OLDS WITH IQs OVER 140 WHO WANT TO GET OUT OF COLLEGE AND BECOME DOCTORS BEFORE THEY HAVE PUBIC HAIR.

30-YEAR-OLDS WHO HAVE 1680 CREDITS TOWARD THEIR BACHELOR'S DEGREE, BUT STILL DON'T FEEL READY TO ENTER THE WORKPLACE.

LH

EVER WISH YOU COULD FLY?
YEAH... THAT'D BE GREAT!
POOF!
WAIT A SECOND...
I DON'T WANT WINGS!!
I WANNA FLY LIKE SUPERMAN, THE HUMAN TORCH AND ALL THEM!
IF MY BUDDIES SEE ME LIKE THIS, I'LL—
HEY, TODD, WHAT'S GOIN' ON IN HERE? WE THOUGHT WE HEARD...
CHECK IT OUT— TODD HAS WINGS!!
HE'S A FAIRY!
HE'S A PIXIE!
AH HA HA HA HA HA
HA HA HA HA!!

START WORKING NOW TO BECOME TIME MAGAZINE'S
"MAN OF THE YEAR"

EVERY YEAR, TIME MAGAZINE NAMES ONE MALE THE MOST IMPORTANT NEWSMAKER OF THE YEAR. WHY NOT MAKE IT YOU?

WHY NOT?

TO WARRANT THEIR ATTENTION, YOU NEED TO BE PRESENT AT EVERY MAJOR NEWS EVENT THIS YEAR.

POLITICAL SPEECHES...

INTERNATIONAL TREATY SIGNINGS...

NATURAL DISASTERS...

AND RIOTS...

TV & STEREO

KOREAN GROCERY

NOW CROSS YOUR FINGERS AND CHECK OUT THE MAGAZINE'S BIG ISSUE!

NEWSSTAND

THOSE JERKS!

TIME
MAN OF THE YEAR
1994
PHYSICIST G.A. SCHMUCK-MAN

THEY WENT AND PICKED SOME BOZO!

YOU COULD PERPETRATE

THE GREATEST HOAX EVER

THE LAST GREAT HOAX WAS THE FAKE REFEREE ON THE FIELD OF SUPER BOWL XXIV, BEFORE THAT IT WAS ORSON WELLES 1938 "WAR OF THE WORLDS" BROADCAST. NOW IT'S YOUR TURN TO PERPETRATE A DEVASTATING HOAX— TO ETCH YOUR INITIALS ON THE TOILET STALL OF HISTORY.

I'M IN! WHAT DO I DO?

YOU'RE GOING TO FOIL THE PLANS OF A PRESIDENTIAL ASSASSINATION BY SUBSTITUTING BULLETS WITH A GAG BANNER THAT HAS "BANG" WRITTEN ON IT.

AWESOME!

FIRST, FIND A RAVING MADMAN WHO'S PLANNING TO SHOOT THE PRESIDENT.

GOT HIM!

NOW, MAKE AN APPOINTMENT WITH THE KILLER FOR THE EXACT PLACE AND TIME OF THE ASSASSINATION.

HOW'S FRIDAY AT 6 IN THE WHITE HOUSE?

FRIDAY'S GOOD. YOU BRING THE GUN.

4H

HERE YOU ARE... HOW'S IT COMING?

I'M HERE, BUT THE ASSASSIN'S LATE!

HE MUSTA FORGOT!!

TOO LATE TO RETHINK IT — THERE'S THE PRESIDENT. YOU'LL HAVE TO SHOOT HIM!

WHICH ONE IS HE? I DON'T KNOW WHAT HE LOOKS LIKE EXCEPT FROM "SATURDAY NIGHT LIVE" SKITS!!

THAT'S HIM—IN FRONT!.

BAM BAM BAM

OH NO! I FORGOT TO SWITCH BULLETS!!

WAIT— IT WAS JUST A JOKE! I DIDN'T MEAN IT!!

64

YOU'VE CRACKED UP YOUR BUDDIES WITH YOUR UPROARIOUS JOKES... NOW IT'S TIME TO TURN YOUR QUICK WIT INTO QUICK CASH, AS SO MANY OTHERS HAVE.

YOU CAN BE A STAND-UP COMEDIAN

GET ON STAGE AND TRY YOUR HAND AT SOME OF THESE CROWD-PLEASING STARTUP TOPICS:

I'VE BEEN DATING A LOT LATELY... LET ME TELL YOU SOMETHING ABOUT DATING...

I'VE BEEN FLYING A LOT LATELY... BOY, THAT AIRLINE FOOD...

BOY, THAT DAN QUAYLE IS SURE SOMETHING...

HA HE HE HO HA

REMEMBER
- MAKE JOKES ABOUT EVERYDAY THINGS WE CAN ALL RELATE TO.
- BREAK UP YOUR ACT WITH A STUNT OR SILLY IMPRESSION— A GUARANTEED APPLAUSE.
- LAUGH NERVOUSLY AT YOUR OWN JOKES. AT LEAST, THEN, **SOMEONE** WILL BE LAUGHING.

FOR A MORE PERSONALIZED ROUTINE, HAWK YOUR OWN DIGNITY FOR A LAUGH → IF YOU HAVE A UNIQUE PHYSICAL TRAIT, TAKE ADVANTAGE OF THE BOUNTY OF SELF-ABASING STEREOTYPE JOKES IT PRESENTS.

OVERWEIGHT

I BOUGHT SO MANY HOSTESS PIES, I BECAME A SENIOR SHAREHOLDER OF THE COMPANY!

GOOFY-LOOKING

WOMEN ONLY WANT ME FOR MY BOD

RACIAL MINORITY

BEING A HISPANIC COMEDIAN IS GREAT— CUZ WHILE WE'RE IN HERE, MY BUDDIES ARE IN THE PARKING LOT STEALING YOUR HUBCAPS

HO HA HA HA HO!   HEE HEE HO HA   HA HO HO HEH

GAUGE YOUR SUCCESS ON THIS STAND-UP COMEDIAN SUCCESS FLOW CHART:

BUST 'EM UP ON OPEN-MIKE NIGHT AT THE LOCAL COMEDY CLUB → HEADLINE AT LOCAL CLUB AMID SEAS OF BELLY LAUGHS → APPEAR ON THE TONIGHT SHOW, USE ALL YOUR BEST JOKES AND GET A WINK AND A THUMBS UP FROM JAY → ADOPT A FUNNY CATCH PHRASE OR ZANY COMEDY STYLE THAT KIDS START MIMICKING IN SCHOOLS NATIONWIDE → SMIRK AND PRATFALL YOUR WAY THROUGH AN HBO COMEDY SPECIAL → DRESS UP IN A BEVY OF HUMILIATING GETUPS IN A BIG-BUDGET COMEDY HIT MOVIE → LIVE OUT THE REST OF YOUR LIFE TRYING TO BE TAKEN SERIOUSLY

30 DAYS TO A SMALLER HEAD

IF YOU'RE TIRED OF THOSE ANGUISHING TAUNTS PEOPLE WHISPER BEHIND YOUR BACK, SUCH AS "WOULD YOU LOOK AT THE SIZE OF THAT GUY'S HEAD," "NOW THAT'S ONE BIG HEAD!" AND OTHER CRUEL REMARKS—AND WHO ISN'T?—DON'T JUST TAKE IT, DO SOMETHING ABOUT IT! AND LET "PLEBES" HELP.

YOUR HAIR CAN OFTEN CREATE THE ILLUSION THAT YOUR HEAD IS 20 TO 30 PERCENT BIGGER— **HACK OFF THAT UNNECESSARY HAIR**

I FEEL BETTER ALREADY!

THE SIZE OF YOUR BODY CAN ALSO CONTRIBUTE TO A DISPROPORTIONATELY LARGE HEAD— **EAT LIKE A GESTATING HIPPOPOTAMUS** UNTIL YOU'VE DOUBLED OR EVEN TRIPLED YOUR BODY MASS

GETTIN' THERE!

YOUR TEETH MAKE YOUR HEAD SUPERFICIALLY 12 PERCENT BIGGER— **REMOVE ALL YOUR TEETH** AND YOUR JAW WILL CLOSE UP TO ONE INCH TIGHTER

HUH! WHAB'YA KNOW!

YOU'VE HEARD THAT 90 PERCENT OF THE BRAIN'S POWER GOES UNUSED... SO WHY WASTE SPACE IN YOUR HEAD HOUSING IT? **HAVE EXCESS BRAINS AND FLUIDS SURGICALLY DRAINED FROM YOUR HEAD**—IT'S A REAL TENSION RELEASER

LASTLY, HAVE A FRIEND **SQUISH YOUR HEAD IN A VISE**... IT MAY HURT A LITTLE, BUT KEEP YOUR THOUGHTS FIXED ON THAT FINAL GOAL!

OH! AAH! OW!!

LOOK AT YOU! LET THEM TRY AND RIDICULE YOU NOW!

THANKF PWEEBF!

SAVE THE EARTH FROM AN ALIEN INVASION!

EVEN YOU CAN HAVE YOUR OWN LATE-NIGHT TALK SHOW!

THEY'RE GIVIN' EM OUT TO ANYBODY WHO'S EVEN REMOTELY FAMOUS:

JOAN RIVERS
RICK DEES
DENNIS MILLER
PAT SAJAK
BYRON ALLEN
RONALD REAGAN'S SON
EVEN JACK LEMMON'S SON!

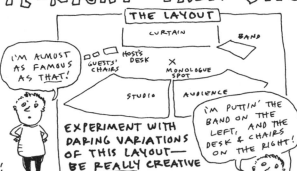

THE LAYOUT

CURTAIN

BAND

GUESTS' CHAIRS — HOST'S DESK

MONOLOGUE SPOT

STUDIO — AUDIENCE

I'M ALMOST AS FAMOUS AS THAT!

EXPERIMENT WITH DARING VARIATIONS OF THIS LAYOUT— BE REALLY CREATIVE

I'M PUTTIN' THE BAND ON THE LEFT, AND THE DESK & CHAIRS ON THE RIGHT!

○ TO FIND GUESTS FOR YOUR SHOW'S FIRST FEW EPISODES, INVITE FAIRLY BIG-NAME SHOW-BIZ FRIENDS WHO STILL OWE YOU A FAVOR.

○ TO FIND A BAND, ASK A MUSICIAN FRIEND WHOM **YOU** STILL OWE A FAVOR.

AFTER YOU'VE USED UP ALL YOUR BEST IDEAS IN THE FIRST FEW EPISODES, STRUGGLE MIGHTILY TO KEEP YOUR SHOW AFLOAT AS LONG AS YOU CAN

TELL REALLY FUNNY JOKES

DAN QUAYLE IS SO STUPID! AM I RIGHT? AM I RIGHT?

KEEP ATTRACTING EXCITING GUESTS

*TONIGHT WE HAVE A GREAT SHOW FOR YA—MY GOOD FRIEND **TODD** IS HERE, AND WE'LL ALSO HAVE A STAND-UP COMEDIAN OR SOMETHIN'*

HOLD ON TO HEAVYWEIGHT ADVERTISERS

BUT FIRST, A WORD FROM YOUR LOCAL NEIGHBORHOOD WATCH PROGRAM

BONUS:

AFTER THEY CANCEL YOUR SHOW, YOU'LL HAVE A CONSTANT SOURCE OF SELF-DEPRECIATING HUMOR FOR THE REST OF YOUR CAREER

JAY, I LOVE YOUR SHOW... NOT EVERYBODY CAN DO THIS— IT'S TOUGH...
I KNOW!

HA HA HA HA HA
CLAP CLAP CLAP CLAP CLAP

DEVELOP YOUR OWN

NATURAL CHARISMA

AND EXERT POWER OVER OTHERS BY RADIATING WINNING CONFIDENCE AND CHARM...

THISSA BE AWESOME!

TO ILLUSTRATE, WE'LL USE CHET, A NATURALLY CHARISMATIC GUY.

HOW ARE YA?

1 TOUCH PEOPLE. THIS PUTS THEM AT EASE YET AFFIRMS THEIR LESSER STATUS.

CHET DEMONSTRATES

TED! GOOD TO SEE YA HOW ARE YA?

NOW YOU TRY

I AIN'A QUEER. HONEST

2 MAKE EYE CONTACT AND STROKE PEOPLE WITH COMPLIMENTS.

CHET

YOU'RE A SMART GUY, TED... I CAN SEE THAT!

YOUR TURN

YOU GOT WEIRD EYEBROWS DUDE!

3 BREAK THE ICE WITH SHARP WIT.

CHET

YOU'RE A DISCO MACHINE AREN'T YA?. I THOUGHT SO—LOOK AT THOSE MOVES!

YOU

...AND THE...OTHER ELEPHANT SAID... NO WAIT! THERE'S A BETTER ONE ON A DIFF'RENT PAGE

NOW YOU'RE READY TO

- MAKE PEOPLE DO WHATEVER YOU WANT
- BECOME A NATURAL LEADER
- INTIMIDATE PEERS
- FRIGHTEN UNDERLINGS

MAKE A CAREER IN...

- CAR SALES
- MID-LEVEL MANAGEMENT
- ORGANIZED CRIME
- POLITICS

BUT IT DOESN'T WORK... HE JUST WALKED AWAY!

LH

78

THE OFFICIAL PLEBES GUIDE TO
GETTING ON TV

DURING A NEWS REPORT

AT THE GAME

IN A CONCERT CROWD SHOT

ON A GAME SHOW

ARE YOUR FRIENDS TALKING ABOUT YOU BEHIND YOUR BACK?

GET IN THE GUINNESS BOOK OF WORLD RECORDS!

IT'S EASY... JUST FLIP THROUGH THE BOOK AND FIND A RECORD THAT WOULD BE A CINCH TO BREAK.

TALLEST NECK: ALL WE HAVE TO DO IS PUT SUCCESSIVE COPPER COILS ON OUR NECKS LIKE CHICKS IN THE KA-REN-I TRIBE.

NA

BIGGEST WEIGHT DIFFERENCE: ALL YOU GOTTA DO IS MARRY SOMEBODY WHO WEIGHS 1300 POUNDS.

NO WAY!

NO, DUDE—JUST MARRY HER TO GET THE RECORD, THEN DIVORCE HER!

OH, YEAH

WAIT, HERE'S A BETTER ONE— **LONGEST TIME STANDING STILL:** THIS GUY STOOD PERFECTLY STILL FOR 73 HOURS!

I COULD DO THAT!

NOW YOU'RE READY TO CALL THE GUINNESS COMPANY TO INVITE ONE OF THEIR OFFICIALS TO WITNESS YOUR RECORD-BREAKING ATTEMPT.

HERE GOES!

AW, FORGET IT—THIS IS BORING!

LTH

YOU CAN BE THE NEXT STEVEN SPIELBERG

(IT'S TIME FOR ANOTHER ONE Y'KNOW)

BEGIN BY MAKING YOUR OWN SCIENCE-FICTION MOVIES— THE GRANDEST EPICS YOU CAN THINK UP. BE SURE TO UTILIZE YOUR FRIENDS. DRESS THEM UP IN CREATIVE COSTUMES

MAKE USE OF THE FAMILY PET IN YOUR MOVIES. AN AFFIXED HORN OR PAIR OF TINFOIL WINGS CAN CREATE THAT OTHERWORLDLY LOOK.

COME HERE, RAOUL, COME HERE, BOY. PLEASE COME HERE, RAOUL... GOD, I'M WASTING SO MUCH FILM

MAYBE WE SHOULD TRY STARVING HIM FIRST

SHOW YOUR MOVIES AT SCHOOL AND AT HOME. EVERYONE SHOULD BE IMPRESSED.

WHO'S THAT?

WHERE'S THAT?

HOW'D YOU DO THAT?

BUT DON'T STOP THERE. RENT OUT A ROOM OF YOUR LOCAL LIBRARY AND CHARGE ADMISSION FOR THE PUBLIC TO SEE YOUR MOVIES.

* SEE * RYKTON THE CONQUEROR AND THE SPACE BANDITS FROM THE EIGHT MOONS OF MYREETHRY!

TICKETS $1

WHY, THIS DISPLAYS AN EXTRAORDINARY AMOUNT OF AMBITION AND SPUNK

WITH YOUR PROFITS FROM THE PUBLIC SCREENING, YOU CAN FINANCE MUGS, LUNCH BOXES, AND T-SHIRTS WITH YOUR CHARACTERS ON THEM.

NOW YOU'RE READY FOR THE BIG TIME

FLY TO LOS ANGELES...

DRESS LIKE A STUDIO EXECUTIVE...

SLICKED HAIR

FAKE MUSTACHE

POSITIVE OUTLOOK

NEW SUIT

NEW BRIEFCASE (CONTAINING BRILLIANT STORY TREATMENTS)

THEN WALTZ RIGHT INTO THE MOVIE STUDIO OF YOUR CHOICE.

THE SECURITY GUARD WON'T SUSPECT A THING.

SOON THE BIGWIGS WILL TAKE NOTICE.

HMM... THIS KID SNEAKED INTO MY STUDIO. THAT DISPLAYS AN EXTRAORDINARY AMOUNT OF AMBITION AND SPUNK. MAYBE I'LL LET HIM RUN FOR COFFEE ON THE SET OF "WHO'S THE BOSS."

ONCE YOU'RE AN IRREPLACEABLE COG IN THE HOLLYWOOD MACHINE, THE INDUSTRY WILL BE YOURS TO MANIPULATE AS YOU CHOOSE....

HOW 'BOUT THIS: AN IMMENSE ARMY OF EVIL ALIEN MONSTERS TRIES TO CONQUER THE EARTH BUT A CUTE FURRY ALIEN AND HIS EARTHLY COMPANION, A TOUGH BUT KIND-HEARTED RETIRED POLICE SERGEANT, DEFEAT THE ALIEN MONSTERS IN A CLIMACTIC BATTLE SEQUENCE BETTER THAN THE ONE IN "MASTERS OF THE UNIVERSE"! A HIT MUSIC SCORE,! A TEAR-JERKER! STUFFED TOYS!

ORGANIZE YOUR OWN
COMMUNITY THEATRE TROUPE

ACTING IS LIFE, AND LIFE IS ACTING, AND LIKE ALL ACTORS, YOU NEED THE THEATRE— WITHOUT IT, YOU WOULD WITHER, CRUMPLE UP, BLOW AWAY AND DIE, LIKE A FLOWER WITHOUT SUNSHINE, ADRIFT FOREVER THROUGH A DARK, LONELY ABYSS.

COULD I, LIKE, GET MY BUDDIES IN ON IT?

— YOU BET!

START BY BUILDING A SIMPLE STAGE ON WOODEN SLATS IN A NEIGHBORHOOD PARK...

CRUDE THOUGH IT MAY BE, YOUR STAGE REPRESENTS THE HIGHEST ACCOLADE OF THE ARTS

SERIOUSLY, GUYS, IF WE REALLY TRY AT THIS, WE COULD END UP AWESOME MOVIE ACTORS EVENTUALLY!

HANGIN' WITH KIM BASINGER AN' THE GUYS IN SLAUGHTER!!

NOW YOU'RE READY FOR YOUR FIRST PRODUCTION!

CHECK OUT A FAMOUS GREEK OR SHAKESPEAREAN PLAY FROM THE SCHOOL LIBRARY AND CAST YOUR BUDDIES IN THE LEADING ROLES...

'TIS THE BETTER... FOR HER... HER, AND SHE BETTER... AND SHE BE NOT, SHE HAS...

GOOD PANDARUS— HOW...NOW, PANDARUS!

OR ADAPT YOUR OWN WORK FOR THE STAGE...

THEY... GOT... BEER... AND... BABES HERE?

FRICK-IN'... AYE...

BUT REMEMBER, FOR YOUR PERFORMANCE, YOUR ACTORS CAN'T READ FROM THEIR SCRIPTS—THEY MUST HAVE ALL THEIR LINES MEMORIZED.

WHAT? COME ON! NO WAY, DUDE

LET'S FORGET THE WHOLE IDEA— THIS IS FOR LOSERS!

BECOME AN ALL-INTELLIGENT LIGHT-BEING
OKAY, I GUESS
PING
IT'S AS THOUGH I'VE BEEN AWAKENED FROM A DEEP SLEEP
EVEN THE CONCEPT OF SELF IS TOO LIMITED TO DEFINE ALL THAT I AM NOW
HEY, TODD! WANNA GO WATCH "PRIVATE SCHOOL" ON DEAN'S VCR?
YOU PROTOPLASMIC AUTOMATONS ARE NO LONGER SIGNIFICANT TO ME
YOU'VE CHANGED, MAN
YEAH- E'R SINCE YA BECAME A ALL-INTELLIGENT LIGHT-BEING
I AM PURE LIGHT, PURE THOUGHT, EMBODYING ALL THE KNOWLEDGE OF THE UNIVERSE
SCREW YOU! WE'LL WATCH PHOEBE CATES' TITS WITHOUT YA!
SLAM
THE MATHEMATICS OF TIME AND ENERGY ARE EXQUISITE
I COULD BASK IN THEIR SIMPLE ELEGANCE FOR AN ETERNITY
WHATEVER HAPPENED TO TODD?
THEY SAY HE MERGED WITH A STAR BILLIONS OF LIGHT YEARS AWAY
FREEZE FRAME!

YOU COULD BE THE NEXT
★ MAYNARD FERGUSON ★

AND JOIN THE RANKS OF KENNY G. AND PETE FOUNTAIN AS ONE OF AN ELITE GROUP OF STAR INSTRUMENTALISTS!

WHO THE HECK IS MAYNARD FERGIS?

KNOWN FOR HIS EAR-PIERCING RANGE AND FLAMBOYANT STYLE, MAYNARD FERGUSON ROSE OUT OF THE BIG BAND / JAZZ SCENE OF THE '50s TO BECOME ONE OF THE MOST POPULAR TRUMPET PLAYERS OF THE '70s.

HUH?

REMEMBER "HEY JUDE"?

YEAH!

HE DID A JAZZY RENDITION OF IT ON HIS 1972 ALBUM, "MF HORN TWO".

REMEMBER "THEME FROM ROCKY"?...HOW ABOUT "THEME FROM BATTLESTAR GALACTICA"?

YEAH

HE BORROWED THOSE TUNES ON "CONQUISTADOR" (1977) AND "CARNIVAL" (1978).

ANYWAY, LET'S GET ON WITH IT— MAKE ME EXACTLY LIKE HIM!

ALRIGHT. FIRST, GET A TRUMPET AND PRACTICE LIKE CRAZY.

BLAT!

SHUT UP IN THERE ALREADY!

THEN, PUT OUT AN ALBUM FEATURING A RENDITION OF A POPULAR THEME FROM 2 OR 3 YEARS AGO.

HOW 'BOUT "THEME FROM T.J. HOOKER"?

PERFECT!

NOW IT'S A CHART-BUSTER AND YOU'RE BEST BUDDIES WITH CHUCK MANGIONE!

WAY TO GO, CAT!

YOU'VE DONE IT! YOU'RE THE NEXT MAYNARD FERGUSON!

OKAY, WHATEVER.

WOULDN'T IT BE EXCITING TO LIVE EVERY MINUTE OF YOUR LIFE WITH THE SAME INTENSE SOCIAL PLEASURE YOU EXPERIENCE IN YOUR FAVORITE BAR? WELL NOW YOU CAN, WITH **YOURSOUND**™, THE NEW PORTABLE BAR-QUALITY SOUND SYSTEM FROM PLEBES ELECTRONICS.

IT'S A **500**-WATT HIGH-FIDELITY LOUDSPEAKER THAT'S AFFIXED TO YOUR HEAD WITH A HANDY BELT STRAP.

RECREATE THE BAR EXPERIENCE IN EVERY FACET OF YOUR LIFE!

— ORDER TODAY! —

94

GO TO COLLEGE FOR FREE!

"PLEBES" BREAKS DOWN ALL THE REASONS YOU GO TO COLLEGE, AND ILLUSTRATES THAT YOU CAN ACHIEVE THE SAME OBJECTIVES **WITHOUT GOING TO COLLEGE!**

LISTEN TO LEARNED PROFESSORS EXPLAIN COMPLICATED IDEAS, PASSING ON THE FRUITS OF THEIR DECADES OF STUDY

WATCH THEM AS GUEST EXPERTS ON CBS NEWS NIGHTWATCH. YOUR COST: ABSOLUTELY FREE!

GET A VALUABLE DEGREE YOU'LL NEED ON YOUR RESUMÉ TO GET A HIGH-PAYING YUPPIE JOB

EASY— WHEN YOU'RE AT KINKO'S TYPING OUT YOUR RESUMÉ, JUST TYPE IN THE DEGREE OF YOUR CHOICE. EMPLOYERS DON'T CALL UP SCHOOLS TO FIND OUT IF APPLICANTS WERE ACTUALLY ENROLLED. AND THEY DON'T ASK TO SEE YOUR DIPLOMA EITHER.

YOUR COST: APPROX. 20¢ (PRINTING, HOURLY MACINTOSH RENTAL)

LIVE LIKE AN ANIMAL IN A FILTHY, CRAMPED DORMITORY WITH COMMUNAL TOILETS

HOLD UP THE NEAREST PRANGE WAY AND WAIT FOR THE POLICE TO COME. SPEND FOUR YEARS IN JAIL.

YOUR COST: NOT A CENT!

ENJOY RIP-ROARINGLY FUN, BEER-BESPLATTERED PARTIES WITH THE WHOLE OF YOUR COLLEGE BUDDIES

WHO KNOWS? AFTER YOU'VE WOWED THEM ALL WITH YOUR STORIES OF A STUDY-FREE TUITION-FREE LIFE, THEY MIGHT JUST PICK UP THE TAB.

YOUR COST: ON THE HOUSE!

LH

PLEBES TIME-MANAGEMENT STRATEGIES

LIKE MOST PEOPLE, YOU SPEND A LOT OF TIME JUST SITTING OR STANDING AROUND DOING NOTHING! JUST THINK OF ALL THE LIFE-ALTERING SELF-IMPROVEMENT EXERCISES YOU COULD PERFORM IF YOU WOULD ONLY HARNESS AND EXPLOIT EVERY LITTLE MOMENT!

WHILE ON HOLD

SCRIBBLE FASCINATING SHAPES ON A PIECE OF PAPER

WHILE WAITING AT THE BARBER

READ PEOPLE MAGAZINE

WHILE RIDING THE BUS

LOOK OUT THE WINDOW — THERE'S A LOT OF STUFF GOING ON OUT THERE!

WHILE STANDING IN THE ELEVATOR

LOOK AT THE FLOOR OR WALL

WHILE WAITING AT THE CROSSWALK

PRESS THE BUTTON FOR THE "WALK" LIGHT AS MANY TIMES AS YOU CAN

WHILE WAITING FOR THE MICROWAVE TO HEAT YOUR FOOD

STAND CLOSE BY AND GET READY TO EAT!

LET'S GO TO VO-TECH

NOT SMART ENOUGH FOR COLLEGE?

WHY NOT LEARN A TRADE AT A TWO-YEAR VOCATIONAL SCHOOL!

IT'S EASY

- WEAR A CAP WITH A HYBRID SEED CO. LOGO ON IT
- WEAR SUNGLASSES FROM WALGREEN'S
- GROW A HALF-ASSED MUSTACHE

I'M GOIN' INTA LAP WELDING!

I'M GONNA CLEAN HEAT SINKS!

COURSE REQUIREMENTS:

HIGH SCHOOL SHOP

LEARN THE "THREE R'S"

1. RESINOUS COMPOUNDS
2. RECALIBRATION OF BLOWPIPE SPLICE PLATES
3. RETENTION OF BITUMEN-INSULATED LEAD HOSING

HM... SEED CAP... SUNGLASSES... MUSTACHE...

YOU'RE ACCEPTED!

YES!

DON'T FORGET YOUR SCHOOL SUPPLIES:

- CHEWIN' TOBACCO
- WORK BOOTS

I GRADUATED IN TWO YEARS AND ONLY LOST ONE FINGER!

PUBLIC SPEAKING

#1 IN THE PLEBES "CONFRONT YOUR FEARS" SERIES

MOST PEOPLE FEAR PUBLIC SPEAKING MORE THAN DEATH ITSELF, BUT YOU CAN OVERCOME THIS FEAR IN 5 EASY STEPS!

1 PREPARE YOUR SPEECH CAREFULLY AND KNOW YOUR SUBJECT.

NO SWEAT! I GOT IT ALL ON 3X5 CARDS! AND i'M A EXPERT ON MY SUBJECT

WHAT'S YOUR SUBJECT?

LLAMAS!

2 YOU'RE READY TO GO... ESTABLISH A RAPPORT WITH YOUR AUDIENCE USING HUMOR.

UH... UM...

EXIT

3 NERVOUS? TRY THIS DAMAGE CONTROL EXERCISE: PICTURE EVERYONE NAKED— THIS WILL SHIFT YOUR DISCOMFORT TO THEM.

UM...

OH NO — i'M SWEATING SO MUCH THE INK ON MY CARDS IS RUNNING!

4 LAST RESORT: READ AS MUCH OF YOUR SPEECH AS YOU CAN, DON'T LOOK UP, THEN RUN OFF THE STAGE.

...SO, IN CONCLUSION... I HOPE YOU KNOW MORE ABOUT LLAMAS NOW THANK YOU GOODBYE!

5 GET CONSOLATION FROM YOUR BUDDIES.

I SUCKED!

IT WASN'T THAT BAD, DUDE!

LH

THIS IS A VERY SERIOUS OFFENSE. WE'RE GOING TO HAVE TO TAKE YOU DOWNTOWN AND BOOK YOU LIKE A CRIMINAL

CAUGHT BREAKING THE LAW?

SMOOTHTALK LAW-ENFORCEMENT OFFICIALS WITH PLEBES' SURE-FIRE, CRIME-BY-CRIME GUIDE TO GETTING OFF EASY.

STRATEGY ONE → DEFEND YOURSELF VERBALLY. TRY THESE INSTANT COME-BACK ZINGERS:

YOUR CRIME →	UNDERAGE DRINKING	VANDALISM	ASSAULT	MASS MURDER
VERBAL DEFENSE →	"C'MON, OFFICER, I WAS JUST HAVIN' A BEER WITH MY BUDDIES!"	"BUT IT'S PUBLIC PROPERTY, AND I'M THE PUBLIC, THAT MEANS I OWN IT!"	"HE STARTED IT!"	"WE WERE HAVING A SPIRITED ARGUMENT AND IT JUST GOT OUT OF HAND."

IS THE OFFICER'S HEART STILL HARDENED? TRY **STRATEGY TWO** → A LITTLE FLATTERY.

YOU'RE IN BIG TROUBLE, SON

OFFICER, MAY I SAY YOU LOOK LIKE A MILLION BUCKS IN THAT FANCY UNIFORM

DO YOU THINK SO, REALLY?

STRATEGY THREE → YOUR LAST RESORT: CRY LIKE A WOUNDED INFANT. THE OFFICER'S INNATE PARENTAL INSTINCTS WILL KICK IN. NO RED-BLOODED OFFICER COULD HELP BUT TAKE PITY ON YOUR NAIVE, ALMOST CHARMING DISREGARD FOR LAW AND ORDER.

OFFICER, PLEASE, (SNIFF) I DIDN'T MEAN TO DO ANYTHING WRONG!

I PROMISE I'LL NEVER EVER DO IT EVER AGAIN!

WELL, I GUESS WE'LL JUST LET YOU OFF WITH A WARNING THIS TIME

THANKS, PLEBES— I OWE YA ONE!

meet... THE DRIVIN'-ALL-NIGHT GUYS

THEY'RE A BUCKET FULL O' LAUGHS — SOMETIMES DOWNRIGHT ZANY!
THEY'RE ON A CROSS-STATE ROAD TRIP IN SEARCH OF GOOD TIMES...

THEY'RE LONG-TIME BUDDIES

DRIVING FOR HOURS THE WHOLE NIGHT LONG.

ONE MINUTE...

LAUGHING LIKE LUNATICS AT THEIR CLOWNISH LATE-NIGHT JOKES.

THE NEXT...

SHARING MEANINGFUL STORIES FROM THEIR PASTS — STORIES OF SADNESS, FRUSTRATION AND PAIN.

ALL TO THE ENERGIZING BEAT OF THE "GOOD DRIVING MUSIC" CASSETTES THEY COLLECTIVELY BROUGHT ALONG.

THEY VISIT PLENTY OF CONVENIENCE STORE/GAS STATIONS

MAKING FUN OF THE SNACK CAKE PRODUCTS AND POST CARD SELECTION.

TRYING TO APPEAR AS COOL, BIG-CITY TRAVELERS TO THE HICK, SMALL-TOWN SALES CLERK.

BUYING ANY OL' ITEM THAT MIGHT SUIT THEIR WHIMSY OR CRACK UP THEIR BUDDY — A PEANUT BUTTER CUP, A DING DONG, A "SHIT HAPPENS" MUG...

LOOK OUT — THEY MIGHT PASS THROUGH YOUR TOWN ONE DAY!

BECOME AN ALL-POWERFUL DEITY!

IT'S AS EASY AS ONE, TWO, THREE!

SURE, YOU'RE JUST AN ORDINARY HUMAN MADE OF FLESH AND BLOOD— BUT WHO'S TO SAY YOU'RE NOT THE EARTHLY VESSEL OF AN OMNIPOTENT SUPERNATURAL BEING?

BOW AND WORSHIP ME— I COMMAND IT!

1 GO TO THE LIBRARY AND CHECK OUT A BOOK THAT LISTS ALL THE RELIGIONS EVER OBSERVED IN HUMAN HISTORY.

GOT IT!

HEY, WAIT— I DON'T HAVE TO READ A WHOLE BOOK TO DO THIS, DO I?

2 NO, JUST SCAN THROUGH IT FOR A LISTING OF ANY OBSCURE GOD THAT MAY HAVE PROPHESIED THE COMING OF A MESSIAH AT A FUTURE TIME.

— HOT DOG! I FOUND SOMETHING.

IT SAYS HERE... GAR-EL-AMAIS-A-MA... A...GOD WORSHIPED... BY INDIAN...FOREST NO-MADS... 10,000 YEARS... AGO...FORETOLD THE...COMING OF...A SAVIOR...

3 VIOLA! YOU'RE A GOD— JUST ANNOUNCE TO THE WORLD MEDIA THAT YOU ARE THAT SAVIOR. YOU'LL BE DENOUNCED AS A FRAUD OR A BLASPHEMER AT FIRST, BUT—

WHAT THE HECK ARE YOU TALKIN' ABOUT? WHERE'S ALL MY OMNIP'TANT POWERS, LIKE THROWING LIGHTNING BOLTS AND STUFF?

YOU WERE JUST LEADIN' ME ON! DOGGONE YOU, PLEBES!!

LH

ARE YOU A BRILLIANT MILITARY COMMANDER?

GREAT MILITARY MEN AREN'T TRAINED, THEY'RE <u>BORN</u>—IT'S IN THE <u>BLOOD</u>. DO Y<u>OU</u> HAVE THE NATURAL ABILITY TO COMMAND THOUSANDS OF TROOPS IN BATTLE?

DO YOU ALWAYS WIN AT "RISK"?

DOES MILITARY HARDWARE MAKE YOUR PENIS TINGLE?

DOES SMALL-GAME HUNTING ALWAYS SEEM TO LEAVE YOU WANTING MORE?

DO YOU ENJOY WRECKING THINGS?

IS MILITARY GENIUS IN YOUR FAMILY HISTORY?

DOES DAD DEVELOP HIS OWN STRATEGIES WHILE WATCHING FOOTBALL ON WEEKENDS?

DO YOU HAVE LARGE AUNTS WHO'VE LEARNED TO USE HUGGING AS A WEAPON?

DOES YOUR GRANDMOTHER HAVE A KNACK FOR UNDERMINING POPULATIONS WITH BROADCAST PROPAGANDA?

TEST YOUR NATURAL LEADERSHIP ABILITY

ROUND UP SOME FRIENDS AND STAGE A CAREFULLY PLANNED SIEGE OF YOUR PARENTS' HOME.

OKAY, NOW SEE IF YOU AND YOUR FORCES CAN OCCUPY YOUR ENTIRE NEIGHBORHOOD!

PLEBES' "TERM PAPER HELPER"

HOW TO WRITE A TERM PAPER WITHOUT HAVING TO THINK

STEP 1

CHOOSE A SUBJECT BY RANDOMLY PLACING YOUR FINGER ON ANY WORD ON YOUR CLASS SYLLABUS

STEP 2

GO TO THE LIBRARY AND CHECK OUT A FEW BOOKS ON THE SUBJECT YOU'VE SELECTED

STEP 3

COMPOSE A ROUGH DRAFT BY PICKING A CHAPTER THAT'S APPROXIMATELY THE SAME LENGTH THAT YOUR PAPER IS REQUIRED TO BE

STEP 4

TAKE EACH WORD IN THE CHAPTER, ONE BY ONE, AND LOOK IT UP IN YOUR THESAURUS. WRITE DOWN A SYNONYM OF EACH WORD, THEREBY REWRITING THE CHAPTER IN YOUR OWN WORDS

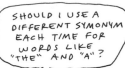

YES

STEP 5

PROUDLY SUBMIT YOUR FINISHED, UNPLAGIARIZED, TYPEWRITTEN WORK TO YOUR PROFESSOR

A SPECIAL FRIDAY NIGHT

WITH NANCY & STEVE

A PLEBES FAIRY TALE

NANCY, WOULD YOU GO OUT ON A DATE WITH ME?

SURE, STEVE... I GUESS

NANCY AND STEVE PREPARE FOR THEIR DATE

NANCY DABS PERFUME IN SPECIALLY SELECTED KARMA POINTS AND NERVE CENTERS ON HER BODY.

STEVE DUMPS A BIT OF COLOGNE ON A DIRTY SHIRT.

GOOD AS NEW!

THEY'RE READY TO GO! AND THOUGH EACH THINKS THE OTHER HAS APPLIED TOO MUCH PERFUMES, THEY POLITELY HIDE THEIR FEELINGS.

YOU SMELL VERY NICE, STEVE

YOU SMELL REAL GOOD TOO

THEY WALK, CLICKITY-CLACK, DOWN THE SIDEWALK IN THEIR SHINY HARD SHOES, TOWARD THE THIRD FINEST RESTAURANT IN TOWN...

JUST "PHASE ONE" OF THEIR EXPENSIVE NIGHT TOGETHER!

THEY BOTH HAVE SPLENDID VISIONS OF TONIGHT'S DATE...

IT WILL BE BEAUTIFUL

MAYBE WE'LL FALL IN LOVE

BUT WHILE THEY DAYDREAM AND MAKE SMALL TALK, THE DANGEROUSLY MIXMATCHED CHEMICALS IN THEIR PERFUMES ARE COMBINING INTO A SEETHING, VOLCANIC BREW OF POWERFUL, SWEET-SMELLING GASES!

IN JUST A FEW SHORT MINUTES, A CHAIN REACTION IN THEIR EPIDERMAL MOLECULES CAUSES THEIR SKIN CELLS TO MUTATE!

SOON NANCY AND STEVE ARE DISFIGURED INTO WHEEZING, WELTING MONSTERS! THEIR SKIN IS PULSATING, BURSTING, AND FALLING OFF THEIR BODIES!

BARELY RECOGNIZABLE AS HUMANS, AND OVERCOME BY MAD, FEVERISH PAIN, NANCY AND STEVE FLEE FROM EACH OTHER...

NANCY SCAMPERS BEHIND A DUMPSTER IN A DARK ALLEY, SCREAMING AND BAWLING AS HER METAMORPHOSING SKIN DRIPS OFF HER HANDS AND FACE.

STEVE SCURRIES INTO A WOODLAND AREA, BELLOWING IN TERROR AND MAKING ODD SEAL-BARKING NOISES THAT ECHO THROUGH A NEARBY VILLAGE, FRIGHTENING THE VILLAGE CHILDREN.

IN TIME, THE SKIN MELTS OFF THEIR BONES, AND THEIR SKELETAL REMAINS SINK INTO THE GROUND, NEVER TO BE SEEN AGAIN.

BACK AT THE RESTAURANT, NANCY AND STEVE ARE LATE FOR THEIR RESERVATION, SO THEIR TABLE IS GIVEN TO SOMEONE ELSE.

PLEBES FASHION UPDATE

STAY ON TOP OF SPRING FASHIONS FOR BOYS BY FOLLOWING THESE SURE-FIRE TIPS:

CAP

BACKWARDS IS STILL COOL, BUT EVEN COOLER IS TO OCCASIONALLY WEAR IT FORWARDS! THERE'S NO BETTER WAY TO SAY "I BUCK THE SYSTEM."

TRENCH COAT

THERE'S SOMETHING UNDENIABLY MYSTERIOUS ABOUT A PIMPLY FACED COLLEGE BUCK IN A DARK TRENCH COAT JUST LIKE HUMPHREY BOGART'S. CHICKS WILL THINK YOU'RE AN INTERNATIONAL SPY WHO STAKES OUT NAZIS BETWEEN PSYCH 103 LECTURES.

SHAVED HEAD

SHAVE A PORTION OF YOUR HAIR IN THE SHAPE OF AN ATTRACTIVE POPULAR ICON. THIS, ALONG WITH YOUR TAN-SPA SKIN COLOR AND FREQUENT CRIES OF "YO, CHILL!" MAY CONVINCE YOUR BUDDIES YOU HANG WITH REAL RAP ARTISTS.

GLOVES

GLOVES WITH NO FINGERTIPS GIVE YOU THE EXOTIC ALLURE OF A REAL HOMELESS PERSON.

BASKETBALL SHOES

AN 80-DOLLAR PAIR SAYS YOU WATCH REAL NIKE ADS.

FOUND YOUR OWN FULLY ACCREDITED COLLEGE OR UNIVERSITY

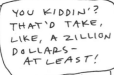

YOU KIDDIN'? THAT'D TAKE, LIKE, A ZILLION DOLLARS— AT LEAST!

LET'S DO SOMETHIN' FUN—LIKE HAVE A BEACH PARTY— WITH GIRLS IN IT!

IT'S EASY. FIRST, BUILD AN IMPRESSIVE-LOOKING CAMPUS...

WHERE'M I GONNA GET ALL THE STUFF TO DO THAT?

THEN HIRE PROFESSORS, ADMINISTRATORS, AND OTHER STAFF PEOPLE...

C'MON— THIS AIN'T FUNNY—THERE'S NO WAY I'M DOIN' THIS!

THEN PRINT YOUR CLASS SCHEDULE AND SEND IT TO ALL THE HIGH SCHOOL SENIORS...

WAIT A SECOND... CAN I, LIKE, MAKE UP ANY CLASS I WANT?

YES. IT'S YOUR UNIVERSITY.

YA MEAN, IT'S COMPLETELY MY OWN—SO I COULD DO WHATEVER I WANT?

THAT'S RIGHT.

BABES 101!! AND BEER! OR WAIT — BEACH PARTY SEMINAR!! NO—BETTER YET— A WHOLE AWESOME BABE DEPARTMENT!

HEY, MTV?...YEAH, I NEED TO HIRE PROFESSORS AT MY NEW UNIVERSITY, SO I'S WONDERIN', LIKE, WHAT'S THE PHONE NUMBERS OF ALL THE HOT-LOOKIN' BABES IN THAT ONE VIDEO...

4H

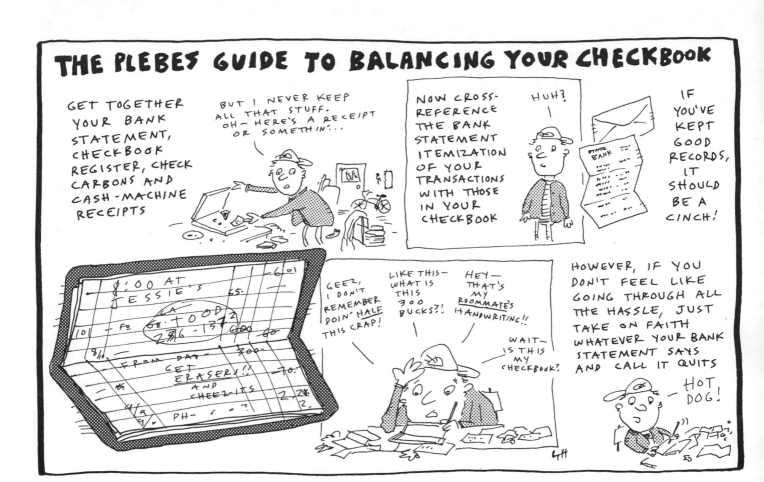

BE A WORLD-CLASS JUGGLER

STEP 1 PRACTICE UNTIL YOU'RE GOOD.

STEP 2 TRY OUT YOUR ACT ON THE STREET.

STEP 3 PERFORM FOR MONARCHS.

4 PERFORM AT THE WHITE HOUSE

AND LOOK— THE PRESIDENT LIKES YOUR JUGGLING SO MUCH, HE'S APPOINTED YOU HIS ONLY WORTHY SUCCESSOR!

NOW YOU'RE THE FIRST JUGGLER TO EVER BECOME LEADER OF THE FREE WORLD!

VANDALISM FOR PENNY PINCHERS

HOW TO DO A LOT OF DAMAGE FOR UNDER $2

THROW AN EGG
IN A CHURCH WINDOW
DURING A WEDDING
OR FUNERAL

NOT ONLY WILL YOU SOIL SOME
POOR SAP'S SUIT, YOU'LL SPOIL A
LIFETIME OF CHERISHED MEMORIES
YOUR COST: ABOUT 10¢

IT DOESN'T COST YOU A CENT TO USE
A ROCK OR SCREWDRIVER TO SCRATCH A
MESSAGE ON THE HOOD OF A PRESTIGE CAR

PUT CRAZY GLUE ON ALL
THE TOILET SEATS IN
THE FEDERAL COURTHOUSE.

WHAT
IN SAM HILL...!

YOUR HONOR,
THE RECESS IS
OVER—WE NEED
YOU IN THE
COURTROOM

WHAT DID
YOU DO—
FALL IN?

YOUR COST: $1.79

EXPLORE OTHER POSSIBILITIES:

SLASH TIRES

CUT WIRING

SQUIRT BLACK
DYE IN THE
CLOTHES DRYER

REMOVE
STOP SIGNS

CAUGHT BY A MEDDLING
AUTHORITY FIGURE?
NO PROBLEM!

HOW WOULD YOU LIKE TO WAKE
UP EVERY MORNING FOR THE REST
OF YOUR LIFE AND FIND...

A DRIVEWAY
FULL OF
NAILS...

A LAWN
FULL OF THE
NEIGHBORS'
TRASH...

A MAILBOX
FULL OF
ASHES...

PLAY THE NEW "PLEBES"

GAMBLE·WITH·YOUR·LIFE·TO·PAY·FOR·COLLEGE BOARD GAME!

FOR KIDS AGES 18-26, FROM FAMILIES WITH INCOMES BELOW $20,000 A YEAR

START HERE

YOU'RE A PROMISING YOUNG HIGH-SCHOOL GRADUATE AND HAVE DECIDED TO EXPAND YOUR HORIZONS BY APPLYING FOR COLLEGE

YOUR PARENTS MANAGED TO SAVE MONEY FOR YOUR EDUCATION ADVANCE TO "YOU MADE IT"

YOUR PARENTS CAN'T AFFORD COLLEGE MOVE AHEAD ONE

THERE'S NO FEDERAL FINANCIAL AID AVAILABLE MOVE AHEAD ONE

YOU MADE IT! YOU GRADUATE, GET A JOB AND BECOME A PROUD, TAX-PAYING AMERICAN CITIZEN... NOW MAKE YOUR KIDS PLAY!

ONE LAST SPIN!

SPIN! SENIOR YEAR!

SPIN!

SIGN UP FOR THE G.I. BILL AND ALL YOUR COLLEGE IS PAID FOR! MOVE AHEAD ONE

SPIN THE "ACTIVE DUTY" FUN WHEEL

SPIN THE WHEEL

ACTIVE DUTY FUN WHEEL

- YOU DIE IN A WAR — YOU LOSE!
- WHEW! THAT WAS A CLOSE ONE!
- LADY LUCK IS ON YOUR SIDE
- THE COLD WAR'S OVER — YOU HAVE NOTHING TO WORRY ABOUT
- IT'S PEACE TIME — YOU'RE IN THE CLEAR
- NO PROBLEM
- CLOSE! BUT NO ACTIVE-DUTY CALL-UP THIS TIME

SPIN THAT WHEEL!

YOU'RE NOW IN YOUR JUNIOR YEAR

GIVE IT A SPIN!

SPIN THE WHEEL!

YOU'RE ENTERING YOUR SOPHOMORE YEAR

SPIN THE WHEEL

50 50 50

LₜH

HOW TO SPOT
THE ADULT STUDENT

DOES SHE...

MAKE SUPERFLUOUS COMMENTS IN CLASS BUT NEVER GET EMBARRASSED?

TALK TO THE PROFESSOR LIKE HE'S A WAITER AT DENNY'S?

GIDDILY DISPLAY A DESIRE TO BE "JUST ONE OF THE STUDENTS?"

BOAST AN UNDERSTANDING OF A CONCEPT BECAUSE OF SOMETHING HER KIDS WENT THROUGH?

LOOK FOR THESE WARDROBE CLUES:

A CONSERVATIVE BLOUSE

A CUMBERSOME NECKLACE

PANTY HOSE

PERFUME YOU MIGHT SMELL IN CHURCH

FINALLY, TAKE A PEEK AT HER NOTES. IF THEY'RE LEGIBLE, YOU'VE SPOTTED **THE ADULT STUDENT**

PLEBES' WORLD OF THE
BIZARRE and the UNEXPLAINED
WAS IT JUST A FLUKE? OR WAS IT...

BLACK MAGIC?

CARL WIZPUT WAS JUST WALKING AROUND RUNNING ERRANDS WHEN HE NOTICED HIS LEFT FOREFINGER WAS BLEEDING FROM A SLIGHT LACERATION.

BUT HE HAD NO IDEA HOW HE'D RECEIVED THE CUT!

PINT-SIZED EVIL FAIRIES?

ELLIE WAMPEK WAS USING AN ORDINARY ROLL OF SCOTCH TAPE WHEN SHE SET IT DOWN FOR A MOMENT TO ATTEND TO OTHER THINGS. WHEN SHE REACHED FOR IT AGAIN, IT WAS GONE!

DEMONIC POSSESSION?

KATE TIMKINS, BACK FROM A NIGHTTIME RUN TO THE BATHROOM, OBSERVED HER SLEEPING BOYFRIEND, TODD, UTTER DISTINCTLY AND INSISTENTLY:

"THE LUMBER YARD IS OPEN TILL 8:30, RIGHT?!"

ULTRASONIC BRAINWAVE-SCRAMBLING BEAMS SENT FROM UFOs?

SID T. McBAFF DIED OF OLD AGE WASHING HIS HAIR IN THE SHOWER!

HE DIDN'T KNOW WHEN TO STOP FOLLOWING THE DIRECTIONS: LATHER, RINSE, REPEAT!

GHOSTS?

JANE DANBUNT WAS WALKING HER DOG, BEAMER, IN THE PARK WHEN ALL OF A SUDDEN BEAMER BARKED AND GROWLED AT A NONDESCRIPT CLUMP OF GRASS!

RUFF! RUFF!

DIVINE INTERVENTION?

MURRAY COSWELL WAS ON HIS WAY TO THE GROCERY STORE, BUT HAD FORGOTTEN HIS LIST. HE REMEMBERED EVERYTHING ON THE LIST EXCEPT ONE THING.

HE PASSED BY A CHURCH AND SUDDENLY REMEMBERED: "FRUIT ROLL-UPS!"

LH

BECOME A GERBIL EXPERT

"I CAN'T WAIT TO START!"

GET AN ENCYCLOPEDIA AND LEARN ALL ABOUT GERBILS! THEN WATCH YOUR LIFE TAKE OFF LIKE A ROCKET!

IMPRESS YOUR FRIENDS...

"COMMON HAMSTERS? WHAT ARE YA—A LOSER? THEY DON'T HOLD A CANDLE TO THE MAGESTIC AFRICAN GERBIL!"

"TELL US MORE! TELL US MORE!"

ADVANCED GERBIL STUDIES

ENCHANT ROMANTIC PROSPECTS...

"OH, SURE, I KNOW A LOT ABOUT GERBILS AND OTHER BURROWING RODENTS, BUT I DON'T WANNA BRAG..."

GERBIL NEWS MONTHLY

INTIMIDATE AUTHORITY FIGURES...

"REV'REND, THE LORD IS TRULY ALL-POWERFUL TO HAVE CREATED SOMETHING AS MAGNIFICENT AS THE ASIAN SAND GERBIL."

TAKE ON THE WHOLE WORLD!

WITH YOUR UNPARALLELED KNOWLEDGE OF GERBILS, BECOME A WORLD-FAMOUS GERBIL EXPERT!

MAKE DISCOVERIES!

WIN THE NOBEL PRIZE!

BUILD YOUR OWN GERBIL TV NETWORK!!

"OH NO— I'VE LEARNED SO MUCH MY BRAIN HURTS!"

PRODUCE YOUR OWN SCI-FI TV SERIES!

FIRST, BUILD SOME REALLY COOL SPACE-SHIP MODELS.

HOW 'BOUT THIS? MY BROTHER'S HAD IT FROM SINCE HE'S A KID

FINE. NOW CUT SOME HOLES IN A PIECE OF BLACK CARDBOARD AND HANG YOUR COOL SPACESHIP IN FRONT OF IT ON A PIECE OF STRING.

GUYS, LOOK! IT'S FLYIN' THROUGH SPACE!

GET OUTTA THE SHOT, DEAN!!

HEY DUDES!

NOW WRITE A SCRIPT FOR YOUR TV SPACE ADVENTURE

WHY? THIS SHIP IS COOL JUST BY ITSELF!

OKAY. NOW GET ONE OF THE NETWORKS TO BROADCAST YOUR SHOW ON PRIME TIME!

SSHH! IT'S ALMOST ON!

ABC PRESENTS THE COOL DEEP-SPACE RANGERS NUMBER 9 SPACE-SHIP SHOW!

GET OUTTA THE SHOT, DEAN!

HEY DUDES!

THAT WAS THE GREATEST TV SHOW EVER!

WOW

NEXT WEEK, COOL SPACE SHIP 9 COMES FACE-TO-FACE WITH A GIANT OUTER-SPACE BEER CAN!

BECOME A CURRENT-EVENTS WIZ

WITH PLEBES' HANDY BECOME-A-CURRENT-EVENTS-WIZ CHECKLIST

CURRENT-EVENTS CHECKLIST

MEMORIZE THIS LIST OF UP-TO-THE-MINUTE NEWS HEADLINES

- THE U.S. GOVERNMENT COMPLETELY SHUT DOWN BECAUSE IT RAN OUT OF MONEY.

- EAST AND WEST GERMANY UNITED INTO ONE COUNTRY.

- THIS SAVINGS & LOAN BAIL-OUT WILL BE VERY COSTLY.

- SOME NEW GUY JUST GOT PUT ON THE SUPREME COURT.

DAZZLE YOUR FRIENDS

IMPRESS YOUR FAMILY

DUMBFOUND YOUR ROOMMATE OR HOUSEFELLOW

'COURSE, NOW, THEY PUT THIS NEW GUY ON THE SUPREME COURT...

SURE, DAD, I KNOW ALL ABOUT THE SAVINGS & LOAN CRISIS — I UNDERSTAND IT WILL BE VERY COSTLY!

HEY, DID YOU HEAR THE U.S. COMPLETELY UNITED INTO ONE COUNTRY? OR NO, WAIT, MAYBE IT WAS...

I'D BETTER TAKE ANOTHER LOOK AT MY "PLEBES" CURRENT-EVENTS CHECKLIST FAST!

START YOUR OWN NEWSPAPER

GET TOGETHER WITH YOUR MOST TALENTED FRIENDS AND GET A GOOD IDEA WHAT KIND OF NEWSPAPER YOU'D LIKE TO PUBLISH...

WE ALL AGREE THEN— A DAILY NEWSPAPER WITH SOPHISTICATED COMMENT, LITERARY CRITICISM, AND POETRY FROM ALL OVER THE STATE

AND BEER REVIEWS!

THINK UP A CATCHY NAME AND ATTRACTIVE MASTHEAD

The Bucky Beacon

YOUR FRIENDS WILL BECOME THE NEWSPAPER STAFF...

WRITER

I GOT A B+ ON MY LAST ESSAY TEST

CARTOONIST

I DREW A PEP RALLY POSTER IN HIGH SCHOOL— A DAMN GOOD ONE!

AD STAFF

HI ED. HOW YA DOIN' TODAY?

FANTASTIC! IT'S GREAT TO SEE YA SID. HOW'S IT GOIN'?

ME? I'M FINE. THANKS A MILLION FOR ASKING CHET. HOW ARE YOU!

SEE HOW MUCH MONEY YOU HAVE ALL TOGETHER AND WORK UP A BUDGET

WE HAVE $750— THAT SHOULD BE MORE THAN ENOUGH TO GET US THROUGH OUR FIRST YEAR

CALL A LOCAL PRINTER TO SEE HOW MUCH IT'LL COST TO PRINT YOUR NEWSPAPER

$800? FOR ONE ISSUE?

TO GENERATE MORE REVENUE, ASK LOCAL MERCHANTS TO ADVERTISE IN YOUR NEWSPAPER

YOU MEAN, YOU THINK WE SHOULD PRINT STUFF THAT PEOPLE WILL REALLY WANT TO READ?

HAVE YOU THOUGHT ABOUT BEER REVIEWS?

HIS FAVORITE MEAL IS "WENDY'S MUSTARD IN A BOWL!"

MEET → **CHARLIE CHEAP**

HE ALWAYS CHECKS THE COIN RETURN IN VENDING MACHINES — WITH A COAT HANGER.

OXIDE AND BLOOD DON'T BOTHER CHARLIE. HE USES DISPOSABLE BIC BLADES TILL THEY'RE A LIGHT BURGUNDY.

HE USES CONDOMS TILL THEY'RE BRITTLE.

HE DOESN'T BUY TOILET PAPER — ANYTHING FROM THE DIRTY LAUNDRY BASKET DOES THE TRICK FOR CHARLIE.

YOU WON'T CATCH CHARLIE SPLURGING ON CAT FOOD. A BIT OF FLY PAPER ON A LEISURELY WALK COLLECTS A TASTY TREAT CHARLIE'S CATS LOVE!

HE ALWAYS CHECKS ASH-TRAYS FOR BUTTS STILL GOOD FOR A PUFF OR TWO, AND GUM STILL GOOD FOR A CHEW OR TWO.

ON A DATE WITH CHARLIE, YOU'LL:

SNEAK INTO A MOVIE THROUGH A REAR EXIT. AND DURING THE MOVIE, CRAWL THE LENGTH AND BREADTH OF THE THEATRE LOOKING FOR COINS.

TIPTOE OUT OF THE RESTAURANT WITHOUT PAYING, AND TAKE A FEW TIPS ON THE WAY.

FORGET THAT NOISY NIGHT CLUB — FISH FOR COINS IN THE GUTTER OUTSIDE USING A LONG STICK AND A WAD OF GUM.

I GOT ONE!

HE STEALS BAILS OF NEWSPAPERS, CLIPS OUT ALL THE COUPONS AND REDEEMS THEM FOR THEIR 1/20¢ CASH VALUE.

LH

THE ROAD TO FINANCIAL INDEPENDENCE

PART ONE: "BREAKING OUT OF THE CYCLE OF POVERTY"

FOR DULLARDS TOO SHEEPISH TO TRY ANY OTHER PLEBES MONEY-MAKING STUNTS

THIS SPECIAL PLEBES PERSONAL-GROWTH CARTOON SERIES WILL SHOW YOU HOW TO BECOME **INDEPENDENTLY WEALTHY** — THAT MEANS LIVING SOLELY OFF THE INTEREST OF YOUR ENORMOUS CASH RESERVES.

BUT LOOK AT YOU NOW...

YOU MAKE BARELY ENOUGH MONEY TO SCRAPE BY

LET'S SEE, 6.50 FOR THE MONTHLY SERVICE CHARGE... OOP— OVERDRAWN AGAIN

HOW WILL YOU SAVE MONEY?

CAN I HAVE A RAISE?

A RAISE?! WE ALREADY GIVE YOU 3.65 AN HOUR FOR CRIPE SAKES!

NOW GET BACK TO THAT DUMPSTER AND SCRUB YOUR LITTLE HEART OUT— I WANT TO BE ABLE TO SEE MY FACE IN IT!

WILL YOUR TOIL NEVER END?

YOUR FIRST IMPORTANT STEP IS TO GET A BETTER JOB.

IF YOU'RE LIKE MOST PLEBES READERS, YOU'RE GUTLESSLY CLINGING TO YOUR FILTHY, DEAD-END SERVICE JOB. YOU NEED TO DISCOVER THE EXQUISITE COMFORT THAT COMES FROM WORKING IN AN <u>OFFICE</u> — A WORK ENVIRONMENT WHERE YOU RARELY SMELL ROTTING REFUSE, DEEP-FRY GREASE OR YOUR CO-WORKERS' SWEAT.

SCAN THE WANT ADS FOR PHRASES LIKE "PICK YOUR OWN SALARY," "UNLIMITED EARNING POTENTIAL," "SALARY PLUS COMMISSION," AND "WILL TRAIN." WITH LUCK, YOU'LL LAND A JOB IN <u>TELEPHONE</u> <u>MARKETING</u>.

(YOUR KEY TO WEALTH WILL BE THE COMMISSION YOU'LL MAKE <u>ABOVE</u> YOUR SALARY)

HELLO, SIR, WOULD YOU LIKE TO SUBSCRIBE TO ANY NUMBER OF FINE NEWS MAGAZINES FOR 40% OFF THE COVER PRICE?... WHY, IT'S 8 A.M. SATURDAY, SIR, WHY DO YOU ASK?

HELLO... MAY I TALK TO YOUR MOMMY OR DADDY PLEASE?... YOUR MOMMY OR DADDY, I SAID... HELLO?... YOU'RE 4 YEARS OLD? THAT'S VERY GOOD!

PLEASE, MA'AM, JUST SAY YES— I NEED TO MEET MY SALES QUOTA THIS WEEK

AT 40 HOURS A WEEK, YOU'LL EARN ENOUGH TO BUILD A GIANT CAPITAL RESERVE IN ONLY 48 SHORT YEARS!

NEXT WEEK: INVESTING IN YOUR FUTURE!

LH

DRAW YOUR OWN CARTOON STRIP
AND MAKE A FORTUNE!

BUY SOME MARKERS AND DRAW SOME CARTOONS THAT ARE REALLY FUNNY

REMEMBER:

YOUR MAIN CHARACTERS SHOULD BE CUDDLY AND LOVABLE SO READERS CAN RELATE TO THEM

SET UP THE JOKE IN YOUR FIRST 2 PANELS, THEN SOCK IT TO 'EM WITH THE PUNCH-LINE ZINGER IN THE LAST PANEL

DRAW IT LARGE SO IT CAN BE SHRUNK DOWN AND PRINTED IN A NEWSPAPER

TEST YOUR DRAWINGS ON YOUR MOST TRUSTED FRIENDS TO GAUGE THEIR OPINIONS

GOOD!

NOW MAKE COPIES OF YOUR WORK AND SEND IT TO YOUR LOCAL NEWSPAPER...

YOU'LL DELIGHT IN SEEING YOUR CARTOONS SANDWICHED BETWEEN THE LEGENDARY COMIC STRIPS YOU GREW UP WITH

SOON YOUR CARTOONS WILL BECOME INSANELY POPULAR!

T-SHIRTS, PEST REPELLENTS AND COMMEMORATIVE BURGER KING DRINKING-GLASS SETS WILL BARE YOUR BELOVED CHARACTERS AND THEIR ENDEARING ANTICS...

A MAJOR NEWSPAPER SYNDICATE WILL GET YOUR CARTOON INTO HUNDREDS OF OTHER NEWSPAPERS...

MAJOR PRODUCT ENDORSEMENTS WILL NET YOU MILLIONS OF DOLLARS!

YOUR CARTOONS WILL INSPIRE "CATCH PHRASES" THAT WILL ENCHANT THE WORLD THROUGH THE POPULAR CULTURE...

YOUR BOOK COLLECTION WILL MAKE THE NATIONAL BESTSELLER LIST... YOUR COLLECTION "TREASURY," "ESSENTIAL" COLLECTION AND "AUTHORITATIVE" COLLECTIONS— JUST REPRINTS OF YOUR OLD CARTOONS— WILL ALL MAKE THE BESTSELLER LIST!!

THIS WEEK, "PLEBES" GETS
ARTY AND EXPERIMENTAL
Coke
Coke
THIS SUCKS!!

THE GRADUATE'S LIFE IN PERSPECTIVE

ALLOWANCE   BIRTHDAYS   PROM   COLLEGE   JOB

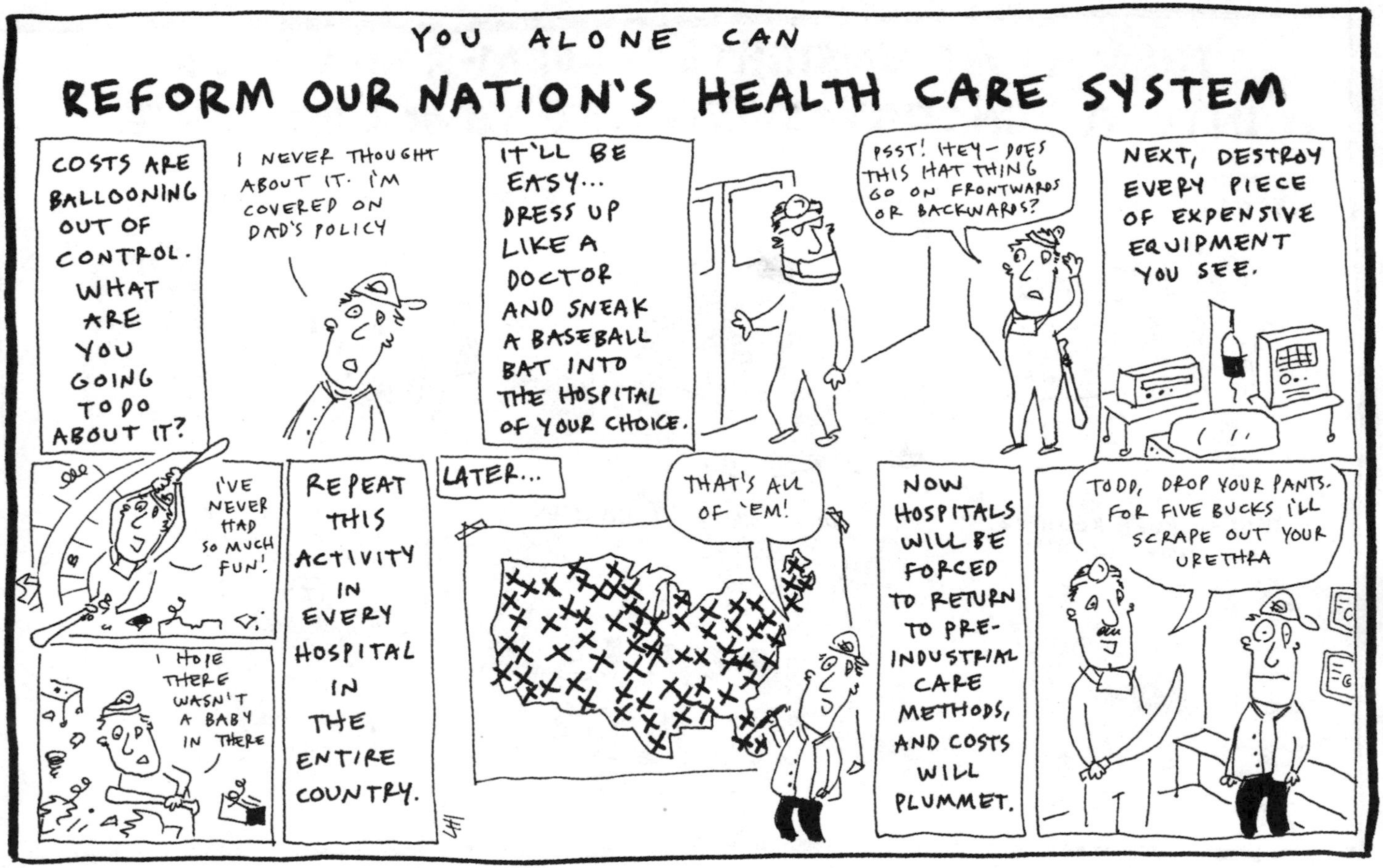
YOU ALONE CAN
REFORM OUR NATION'S HEALTH CARE SYSTEM
COSTS ARE BALLOONING OUT OF CONTROL. WHAT ARE YOU GOING TO DO ABOUT IT?
I NEVER THOUGHT ABOUT IT. I'M COVERED ON DAD'S POLICY
IT'LL BE EASY... DRESS UP LIKE A DOCTOR AND SNEAK A BASEBALL BAT INTO THE HOSPITAL OF YOUR CHOICE.
PSST! HEY—DOES THIS HAT THING GO ON FRONTWARDS OR BACKWARDS?
NEXT, DESTROY EVERY PIECE OF EXPENSIVE EQUIPMENT YOU SEE.
I'VE NEVER HAD SO MUCH FUN!
I HOPE THERE WASN'T A BABY IN THERE
REPEAT THIS ACTIVITY IN EVERY HOSPITAL IN THE ENTIRE COUNTRY.
LATER...
THAT'S ALL OF 'EM!
NOW HOSPITALS WILL BE FORCED TO RETURN TO PRE-INDUSTRIAL CARE METHODS, AND COSTS WILL PLUMMET.
TODD, DROP YOUR PANTS. FOR FIVE BUCKS I'LL SCRAPE OUT YOUR URETHRA

YOUR LIFE FLASHES BEFORE YOUR EYES

COURTESY OF PLEBES

MARKET YOUR PRODUCT FOR KIDS!

KIDS ARE BLANK SLATES—THEY'LL BUY ANYTHING IF THEY THINK THEY'RE SUPPOSED TO. **CASH IN ON THIS ADORABLE TRAIT WITH MARKETING!**

HAVE YOU GOT A WINNING PRODUCT IDEA?

NOTHIN'—JUST THIS PARTIALLY CRUSHED BEER CAN

YOU CAN IMPROVE UPON YOUR IDEA IN TWO WAYS: FIRST, RE-NAME IT.

YEAH, OKAY... IT AIN'T A BEER CAN, IT'S A MICHAEL JORDAN ACTION FIGURE THAT FOLDS INTO A ROBOT, NINTENDO CASSETTE, AND FRUIT-FLAVORED ZOTS DISPENSER!

SECOND, PACKAGE IT CLEVERLY.

HEY—YOU'RE RIGHT! IT LOOKS A LOT BETTER IN THIS LUNCH BAG!

NEXT, PUT ADS ON SATURDAY MORNING TV. USE ICONS AND LANGUAGE KIDS CAN RELATE TO.

CHECK IT OUT! MY SPOKESMAN'S A RAPPIN' DINOSAUR!

RADICAL!

YOU'LL ALSO NEED A BREAKFAST CEREAL.

THAT IS RADICAL!

NEW
Michael-Jordan-Action-Figure-that-Folds-into-a-Robot-and-Nintendo-cassette-and-Fruit-Flavored-Zots-Dispenser
Bits

SO I'M DONE, RIGHT? I MADE A FORTUNE AND CAN NOW RETIRE.

THERE'S MORE—IN 20 YEARS, NOSTALGIA FOR YOUR PRODUCT WILL MAKE YOU **ANOTHER** FORTUNE!

WHO CARES? I'LL BE TOO OLD TO SPEND IT BY THEN

146

DANCE THE NIGHT AWAY!

LEARN ALL THE LATEST STEPS AND BE THE STAR OF THE DANCE FLOOR!

THE FOXTROT...
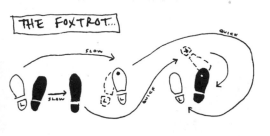

THE RUMBA!

THE VIENNESE WALTZ

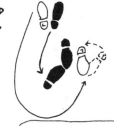

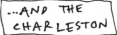
...AND THE CHARLESTON